OUTBOX FROM INNER SPACE

Selected Poems by Christopher Payne

Published by New Generation Publishing in 2014

Copyright © Christopher Payne 2014

First Edition

The author asserts the moral right under the Copyright, Designs and Patents Act 1988 to be identified as the author of this work.

All Rights reserved. No part of this publication may be reproduced, stored in a retrieval system or transmitted, in any form or by any means without the prior consent of the author, nor be otherwise circulated in any form of binding or cover other than that which it is published and without a similar condition being imposed on the subsequent purchaser.

www.newgeneration-publishing.com

 New Generation **Publishing**

Edited by Sophie Heason

*For my wife, Paddy Payne,
With love and gratitude*

Foreword

What was in your Outbox this morning? What have you been sending out into the world? In this beautiful birthday selection of Christopher's poems we gratefully receive what he is dispatching, and we learn where it comes from – from inner space!

But what goes out must first come in, and actually these poems give privileged insight into Christopher's spiritual Inbox. And what a vibrant collection of sources he has – his inspirations arriving as they do from so many different places, people, experiences, memories and prayers.

We are privy to a secret communion celebration among underground Christians in a country where their faith is banned. A long-dead Carmelite nun sings us her song of commitment. Children with sticky fingers also leave a trail of their indestructible sense of wonder.

We stand by, in sorrow, as ' Mum' inexorably slips away through her closing years and days, and we witness the deep empathy of a doctor who listens as his patients spill out their stories 'at first acquaintance'.

The luminescence of a quantum universe, alive with mystery, irradiates 'Hugh' and his home-grown tomatoes and we recognise each of these realities to be a unique and irreplaceable part of God's unfolding kingdom.

So let Christopher carry you to where God and humanity meet and embrace, as the meridian light beam shines out from Greenwich, directing our hearts to the True North of God's presence within us.

Margaret Silf
November 2013

Introduction by the Author

Outbox From Inner Space

This Birthday Collection, made possible by my loving family, celebrates ten years of Creative Writing, poetry which has reached the Outbox with an imperative to be shared.

There is frequently a strong sense of a source, reaching an inner space that can be described as sacred. An awareness of the Holy Spirit brings experience and the witness of the Bible together.

Chapters Two and Three contain my first two, short Collections, published by Feather Books. I have included the Foreword to each, kindly contributed by Margaret Silf, the ecumenical author of the influential 'Sacred Spaces – Stations On A Celtic Way' (Lion). Acknowledgements and Notes on these two chapters may be found at the end of the book.

Over the past few years the Men's Group at St. James's Church, Kidbrooke, has met regularly and I have taken the minutes of these meetings in various poetic forms, sometimes in a lighter vein. Chapter Four, 'Taking The Minutes', contains some examples.

Paddy and I have been blessed with four daughters and nine grandchildren, inspiring verse featured in Chapter Five.

As a Londoner, many of these poems have been written here and Chapter Six include an item from Bermondsey, where I worked for 24 years; from our home in Kidbrooke; and from Deptford. After retirement I became a volunteer at Deptford Churches' Centre (now known as 'Deptford Reach') www.deptfordreach.org.uk particularly enjoying the music and poetry workshops and performances led by professionals from the charity 'Create' www.createarts.org.uk

The final two chapters include work completed at events with the 'Creative Arts Retreat Movement' www.carmretreats.org on holidays and other journeys.

Many thanks are due to my strongly supportive family, especially Sophie Heason for editing, and Matt Heason for

computer and technical expertise   including cover photography
www.heason.net

also www.christopherpaynepoetry.net my website.

Ten of these poems appeared in the Anthology 'Poets At The Priory', published by Christchurch Priory, Eltham, London, in 2013.

Finally, grateful thanks to New Generation Publishing   for advice and encouragement.

Table Of Contents

Foreword 7
Introduction by the Author: 9
Table Of Contents 11
Chapter 1 17
Outbox From Inner Space 17
   A Secret Code For Christmas 17
   A Splinter In The Palm 18
   After Prayer 19
   Aylesford Psalm 19
   Do We Believe In The Holy Spirit?… 19
   The Elizabeth Trilogy: 20
   1. Hymn: Be You My Sanctity 20
   2. Elizabeth Of The Trinity 21
   3. January The Twenty-First 22
   It Will Look Like This… 22
   Lady In Waiting 22
   Late Night Sermon 23
   New Wineskins For Corrymeela 24
   November Beech 24
   Out There 24
   The Glory Of The Humble Things… 25
   The True Vine 26
   Waiting 26
Chapter 2 28
Incarnate! 28
   Foreword 28
   Author's Introduction 29
   Incarnate! 30
   A Good-will Offering 30
   A Song From The Cross 31
   Before Christmas 31
   Beyond The Decorations 32
   Glory To God In The Haiku 33
   Mid Winter Crisis 33
   Good Morning, Hello And Welcome 33
   Confession 34
   The Word 34
   The Creed 35
   The Offertory Procession 35

    Karaoke Christmas 36
    Reunion 36
    The Ballad Of Joe And Mary Church 37
    The Emptying... 39
    The Knife Edge 39
    The Night The Poetry Caught Fire 40
    The Perfect Day... 41
    The Personal Rainbow... 42
    Without Christmas... 43
Chapter 3 44
A Heart For Mission... 44
    Foreword 44
    A Heart For Mission - Metre 8 7. 8 7. D Trochaic.... 45
    A Hill Of Beans For Peace 45
    And A Middleton New Year 46
    Before The Diagnosis.. 46
    Blueprint In The Sand 47
    Day One... 48
    Dear Colleague 48
    From Galilee To Here.. 49
    Hold That Word 50
    God, Forsaken (A Meditation On Psalm 22)............. 50
    Hopton Wafers Churchyard....................................... 51
    How Was Your Day? 52
    Iran Morning 53
    Lord, Teach Us To Pray - Metre 13 10 13 10 53
    Michaelmas 54
    Palms Of Jericho 55
    Paradox.. 55
    Prayer Tank 56
    Stay Close.. 56
    Taking The Oath.. 57
    To See More Clearly 57
    Twelve Epiphanies 58
    Yellow 59
Chapter 4 61
Taking The Minutes 61
    A Hard Debating We Had Of It................................. 61
    A Globe Theatre 62
    Dining Room Three... 63
    (With acknowledgements to Rupert Brooke)............ 63
    Genesis 3 In Lent... 63

    Global Mourning : A Microcosmic Event 64
    Home Grown Toast 65
    Intelligent Design 65
    Just Another Day In The Wilderness 66
    Lord, Draw Near… 67
    Pitter-Patter Noster 68
    Max's Tale 69
    Social Climbing 70
    The Cry On The Street 71
    The Dashing 'Why Start?' Rant 71
    The Kidbrooke Beatitudes 72
    The Padre 73
    The Verse 73
    The Very Idea 74
    To The Ed. 74
    We Three 75
Chapter 5 76
Family And Other Blessings 76
    February The Fourteenth, 2001 76
    A Sunny Hillside In Brentwood 76
    Autumn Song For Ciara 78
    Best Friends And Brothers 79
    Blue Crocuses 79
    Bryn 80
    Coliemore Harbour 80
    Crowberry Lane 81
    Dylan 82
    For Dorrie, From Her Son 83
    For John Of The North 83
    On The Footpath To Sewardstone Marsh 84
    Sandals And Boots 84
    Spring-Green Spruce 85
    The Way We Were 86
    Together 86
    24.8.1918 87
    St Andrew's Day, 1969. An Edinburgh Festival 87
    You're 89, Mum 88
Chapter 6 90
From London With Love 90
Bermondsey 90
    At First Acquaintance 90
Deptford 92

By Whose Authority?..92
Ukulele Rock...93
Ode To An Ode 94
Ode To A Toy Cat...94
'And Stay Out!…'..94
Ambiguity Rules Twice...95
Blue Fingers 95
Cinquains From Art..96
Crime Scene?...96
Desert Island Discos..96
Hope 97
Hurricane Cheryl Hits Deptford 97
Journey Through the Centre 97
Meridian At Nightfall..98
My Deptford...98
Rose in full bloom 99
A Doorstep On A Roman Villa 99
Six Characters In Search Of An Emotion.........................99
The Art Room And The Senses......................................100
The Door To Number 47...100
The Gifts..101
Through His Pockets 101
Kidbrooke...101
Every Millennium Eve, It's Just The Same....................101
Kidbrooke..102
We Don't Have Bonfires..102
And Again I say, Recycle..103
Crescendo 104
London's Water-colour Air..104
Chapter 7 105
Journeys...105
A Family Of Adopted Oak And Pine… 105
At The Ramblers' Tea Room 105
Beware Of The Chickens 106
His Environment 106
A Paphos Trilogy 106
1.Tell Me, Paul..106
2. Apostolic Succession...106
3.Inter Faith Dialogue...107
Points Of View 107
Shadows On The Sands 107
Since The Year of The Flood… 107

  St. Denys's Sundial 108
  The 11.15 From Didcot Parkway 108
  The Jurby Deodand 108
  What Did You Go Out To See? 110
  World Cup, Japan, 2002 111
  The Visitor And The Madonna 111
  Twelve Stone Blocks 112
  Orzola Harbour 113
Chapter 8 114
Earlier… 114
  The Golden Arrow 114
  A Small Bereavement 114
  Wine and Incense - A Love-Offering. 115
  Acrostics 116
  Beside The Traffic's Roar 116
  Daughter Of The Totem 117
  Dearest Clone- A Mother's Promise 117
  Extra-ordinary 118
  From Life 118
  Give Us Today 119
  Haiku 1 - Sam, About Tom 119
  Haiku 2 - Alpha To agemO 120
  Haiku 3 –Encounter 120
  In All Its Fullness 120
  Ingrate 120
  Pearls Or Beads 121
  Plane Trees... 121
  Poetry In The Rain 122
  Post Meridiem 122
  Rydal 122
  Sequel 123
  Set Aside… 123
  Shimmer 123
  These Are The Days 124
  Train Journey 125
  Vocation 125
  When Will They Ever Learn? 126
  Your Early Morning Call 126
Acknowledgements And Notes 127
  Chapter 2 127
  Chapter 3 128

Chapter 1

Outbox From Inner Space

A Secret Code For Christmas

My chopsticks raise a little rice
And dip it in the sweet and sour sauce
I lift brown eyes and catch your glance
Across the crowded room.
We share the secret Communion of our Lord
Until He returns.

My glass reflects the lanterns
In the restaurant as I sip in memory
And catch again your eye across the rim;
A secret toast the Party still forbids
To Jesus and to freedom
When He returns.

My tag is there upon the cavern walls
Graffiti in the catacombs of Rome.
In those days I was fair, my eyes were blue
An 'angel' brought by slave ship from the north.
You may still see my 'X', 'Chi', code for Christ
Wishing you 'Happy Xmas' till He returns.

The meaning of my code is plain to see
For those who know the legends of the past.
With Holy Communion banned, the bread and wine
Could be replaced between us by the food
We shared in public places, private prayers
Exchanged in dangerous hopes of His return.

I am the secret Christian. Through the years
My faith has had to be behind closed doors
Or underground where symbols still survive.

The Greek initial for the expected Christ
Became in English 'X' which marked the spot
Where many races prayed for His return.

A Splinter In The Palm

A Tehran street in '72.
Warned of the traffic, I took care
As dusty, morning sun broke through.
In January Customs Halls
The interpreter had been my guide
With Mission Guest House early calls.
Negotiations of the fees
Were safely done, one task remained
That last morning. Beneath bare trees

I watched the distant traffic light
Which still showed red. I crossed alone
And then recalled my daughter's voice
When first we landed in the night
'Look, Dad, they're driving on the right!'
And instantly a rushing wind
Provoked a reflex backward step
A speeding wooden-sided van
Grazed my left hand raised in salute
And disappeared back into time
While I stayed to pursue the plan.

The street a desert wide and cold
Behind me caught my thoughtful eye
How many millimetres from
The company that grow not old?

I took a splinter from my palm
Like carpenters since Roman days
And set out to complete the task
Gratefully in memoriam.

After Prayer

Help me to put action where my prayers are.
Help me to live differently and climb another stair
Building slowly
Making progress
Not forgetting past forgiveness
Revelations and the fact that you are there.

Aylesford Psalm

To you, O Lord, I lift up my voice:
How can I keep silent
Now my deafness is ended?

In your unfailing love you did not desert me:
Through the busy years
Of unthinking inattention.

Through the decades of heavy feet:
Trudging, not leaping,
From the dusty pavements.

Now my soul longs to fly with your praise:
And your music calls to me
In the distance.

How can I share these glimpses of your glory?
Give me your words
That I may join in the chorus.

For the rehearsal is over:
Your hand raises the baton.

Do We Believe In The Holy Spirit?…

The Breath of God ruffling our hair
As we kneel in worship or in grief,

The Wind of God filling our sails
Though we tack and turn to resist the divine intention,

The Voice of God whispering in our ears
When we would prefer Earth's tremors or the storm,

The Fire of God refining our lives' metallic ore
Until true selves become fit for eternity,

The Flame of God lighting the lanterns
For us to hold high as we stumble along,

The Sound as of many waters of refreshment
Cascading from the Source in the City of God,

The Spring of living water bubbling from our hearts
In rare moments abandoned to tongues of praise,

The Muse in early morning urging
Us to write and dance to His tempo,

Holy healing, wholeness and re-creation
Preparing us for the coming day of prayer?

The Elizabeth Trilogy:
1. Hymn: Be You My Sanctity - Metre 10 11. 11 11. [12]
(Based on the writings of the Carmelite nun, 'Elizabeth of the Trinity', 1880-1906)

Be you my Sanctity, my risen Lord
May we share the strength that your Heaven can afford
O, come, Holy Trinity, dwell here with me
May we dance in Unity, O Glorious Three.

Be you my Sanctuary, I give you my life
With Christ it is hidden in God, where the strife
And the struggle is silent in this sacred place

Where Heaven is within us as we seek your Grace.

Be you my Paradise, garden of peace
Where prayer has a purpose may praise never cease
On behalf of a world without love of their own
My Friend and my Father, I worship alone.

Image of Trinity, God in our hearts,
In love, prayer and silence eternity starts
As we find you everywhere, singing your song
Alone or together, with you, Three in One.

2. Elizabeth Of The Trinity

How far away she seems, this blessed nun.
Barely a century ago she lived and died
For Christ; a Carmelite enclosed
In Dijon, Catholic House besieged
By secular Republic of La France.

And yet we can still see the world
She knew beyond the veil. Letters and family
Photographs reveal the beauty
Of the Army daughter, devoted to her home
And younger sister. Marriage prospects beckoned
And a promising concert pianist career.
She knew God even in her fingertips.

Steadfast, her early teenage vow to chastity
Her deep preoccupation with the nearby convent
But above all her love affair with God
Compelled her to the choice to leave the world
Behind closed doors, while still involved in prayer
For all outside those walls.

Always her focus was elsewhere. She lived with God
As with a friend, surrounded by
The gentle chimes of Carmel.

3. January The Twenty-First

What joy! My Wedding Day. His bride at last.
My life-long longing now fulfilled at Agnes-tide
As I receive my bridal veil of black.
This is my lovely day, the day I shall remember
The day I'm dying, allow me this.

Our empty cross, our cell together
We are prisoners of love, behind these grills
Within our soul, our cell within a cell.
Our only housekeeping will be in this community
And yet our married bliss
In silence and in prayer
Our light, our love, our life, this we will share.

It Will Look Like This...

...Through the glass darkly,
The Corinthian mirror burnished bronze
Imprinted with the loving donor's face
Whose features coincidentally appear
Amongst my own.

Lady In Waiting

(with acknowledgements to T.S. Eliot)

There will be a birth, certainly,
Also a death
And will it be
Satisfactory?
The point of this waiting, this 'now',
Is the uncertainty, not yet knowing,
Hoping for the best, fearing the worst.
Both have been familiar, in Nazareth.

Then there is the journey.

No camels, no servants to run away.
A falling among thieves?
Becoming lost in the travelling crowd
Of pilgrims to ancestral sites of harvest fields?

And the gifts.
Grace, love and trust, already.
Gold and worship incense in the heart for now.
Please, God, not myrrh, not yet.

We know and can recite his name,
Like cousin John, signifying purpose.
If he will save, then surely he must live?

His first death, from the waters, will be deliverance
From glory to Earth,
From creative power to passive birth.
Then will we see him face to face,
And rejoice, that a son has been born
Into the world?

Late Night Sermon

John 3 and verse 16 his text
The preacher from another culture
Unembarrassed standing before strangers
'I have to do this', he said
And told us of the love of God.
He was nervous. 'Some of us'
He sweated out, 'Have had a bad day'.
The theme developed moderately well, as he
Referred to Hell, too soon, but then recalled
How Jesus died to save us.

After all, it was the week of Resurrection
But then the captive congregation, unaccustomed
To such African directness of approach
Started to intervene. 'Give it a rest, mate!'

'I'm trying to have a nice little sleep here!'
'Tell 'em in the next carriage!'

He didn't take the hint. Hostility about
To replace cheerful London tolerance of difference
I shuffled past, alighting at my stop
Composing fantasies of brave support.

New Wineskins For Corrymeela

Step by step
Guidelines Applied.
Raw edges
Exposed and
Stitched up
Recovered.
Scorched
Loose ends
Gently
Gathered
Now conform to a pattern.

November Beech

Like a cloud of witnesses
The beech leaves startled from their wind-blown tree.
All Summer they had waited
For this momentary parable and me.
They drily crackled settling on the grave
Their coppery goodness offering back their sunshine gifts
Beside the rose we gave.

Out There

Come out of your buildings
Let the walls disappear
That divide you from others
Who are longing to hear
The tale of redemption

The voice of their King
The good news He will bring.

Throw open your windows
And breathe the fresh air
Of the Spirit of freedom
Rejoice with Him there.
Are you feeding the hungry
The lambs of the Lord
With the milk of His Word?

The city is waiting
For churches to share
The love of their Father,
To give hope for despair.
Being part of the answer
Responding to prayer
We will find Him
Out there.

The Glory Of The Humble Things…

…Of roundabouts and slides and swings
And toffee apples, sticky hands
Or spades and buckets on the sands

Should not be lost with growing-up
Through sarcasm or showing-up,
Humiliation (cf.humble)
By those who wish to see you stumble.

A little child enters the Kingdom
By way of Hopkins' 'thingy thingdom',
A sense of wonder, artless charm
And never knowingly causing harm.

The Christmas angels' symphony
Is followed by Epiphany

A showing-forth, reality
A sound-bite of true quality.

The True Vine

The wine of the Kingdom
Makes glad the heart of mankind.
The grapes of the vineyard
Are the fruit of faithfulness.

The tendrils, seeking to hold fast like a baby's fingers
Stretch out in longing towards sunshine blessings.
The leaves in a mosaic of receiving
Are evidence of life rising from the Source.

The dry and peeling bark protects
Tender channels, flowing with the Spirit.
The stem is gnarled and sculpted with age
From a long life of pruning and fresh starts.
The roots disappear into the sands of time
And drink deeply from living water.

The gardener labours with a Father's care
The branches work, contributing their share
The vine, the Lord, new Israel's truest wine will bear.

Waiting

The serenity with which we face death
Must be practised beforehand.
The equanimity with which we meet God
Is for here and now.
He doesn't wait until the end to be real to us.
There is a longing in His heart
For us to share the powerlessness
Which is the expression of His utmost power.

We need not wait until the end

To know His presence.
Our stillness before Him and the beauty
Which He has prepared for us to experience each day
Are the gifts for this moment
And the promise of courage to come.

Chapter 2

Incarnate!

Foreword

Advent catches us up each year into a space of waiting _ waiting for slow, silent growth to manifest itself in a new springtime, waiting for old wounds to heal and promises to be fulfilled. Yet, so often, and for so many, there is a barrier between where we are and the space into which God beckons us. The barrier is made up of 'the decorations' – the inconsequential things that preoccupy us, take over our conscious minds and screen out the greater vision that is unfurling in a humble stable in a little town in the Middle East.

In this beautiful collection of poems, Christopher takes us 'beyond the decorations' and draws back the veil to reveal a glimpse of that mystery that becomes incarnate in the stable and continues to become incarnate in the moment-by-moment experience of our own lives. He invites us to enter through the doors of human time and ordinary experience into a realm of timelessness, where the greatest promise of all is being fulfilled, and where, in the fullness of God's love, we will become the people God is dreaming us to be.

Margaret Silf Advent 2007

Author's Introduction

The first word of the first poem in this Collection is 'Jesus'. He is the starting-point.

Without Christ, without Christmas, many of us would have led different lives. Our faith originates here, in a historical Person whose human milestones, life events and teachings about His Father in Heaven immediately bring us face to face with paradox.

Poetry and prayer have recently helped me to deal with paradox and to reconcile apparent contradiction.

The title poem is 'Incarnate!' That exclamation mark expresses the surprise, the wonder, the sheer joy experienced in contemplating the implications of 'Incarnate God, new mystery…'. God's command is 'Let there be Incarnation!' His new idea now enters into history.

!

Incarnate!

Jesus was once six weeks old,
The smile of God upon His world
Was never seen until that day
And now it never fades away.

Jesus was once eight days old,
The quick, sharp knife, her blood ran cold,
Mary's tears gave her away,
God's blood was first shed on that day.

Jesus was once minutes old,
The umbilical cord will hold
Eternally on mothers' hearts.
God's life as one alone now starts.

Jesus was once eighteen weeks old
From His conception; arms would fold
And legs would kick within the womb,
For God there was no other room.

Jesus was once one second old,
Annunciation could be told,
Incarnate God, new mystery,
Now enters into history.

Jesus was once, and is again,
Infinite, timeless, yet for men
And women shared seconds, weeks, days.
We cannot understand, just praise.

A Good-will Offering

God wills good to all He has created
All the best, a cheery greeting at the birth of Love incarnate.
Angels sang of Glory and good-will
As attributes of God. His love

Spreads over the night sky and down to Earth
Where we are loved for ever
Unconditionally and with grace
Which tells of undeserving.

A sadness at the centre of this love
Must be the unrequiting
Not returned even if known
Not acknowledged even if heard
Brushed like crumbs to one side even if observed
But to those who reach out in response,
The Kingdom.

A Song From The Cross

A song-thrush on St. James's spire
Singing with all his might
A clarion call to worship God
With joyful voice and flight

Of fancy and imagination
Swelling speckled throat
With praise and clarity and tunes
Of glory in each note.

The gardener pointed him out
So high above the town
Perched on the cross almost unseen
While liquid song flowed down

To lift our eyes to seek the source
Of beauty lost in praise,
Once seen our spirits will return
To join and sing and gaze.

Before Christmas

Will He be here before Christmas?

Will the Advent hope be fulfilled?
Do we trust in His love when Earth's kingdoms fall
At His gentle word of command?

Will it all be over before Christmas?
Will the whole rigmarole be stilled?
At the end of the fast will the Bridegroom call
For lamps held high as we stand?

Will we welcome Him back before Christmas?
Will the promised strength He willed
Be ours to grasp this year above all
As we greet Him hand in hand?

Beyond The Decorations

Beyond the decorations
Sits an altar, empty, waiting
For the coming of the Host, the Son of God
In bread and wine.
As we approach in expectation
Of the memorial's fulfilment
Then God's Spirit brings His presence
To our hearts, to yours and mine.

Beyond the decorations
Stands a chair, still empty, waiting
For the coming of the Judge, the King
Our Shepherd, Friend divine
So we'll watch in expectation
Salvation history's fulfilment
When God's angels sing His glory
In our hearts, in yours and mine.

Beyond the decorations
Hangs a wreath of holly, waiting
Like a crown of thorns, the green and red
The torture of the Vine

But we see the coming Advent
As the risen Christ's fulfilment
Of the promise of the Gospel
To our hearts at the end of time.

Glory To God In The Haiku

Angels have their harps
So they may praise Him in tune.
Flat angels, flat Earth.

Mid Winter Crisis

What shall I give Him
Rich as I am?
If I were a shepherd
My finest ram
 If I were a wise man
Experience impart
But all I am I give Him
The sacred space within my heart.

Good Morning, Hello And Welcome

 Why are we here
Today? Why did we come
To church, today?

Perhaps it is our custom
Every week or every
Now and then
To come, recalling services from times
Gone past and seek to live again
The long-remembered days
Of blessing and closeness to God.

Perhaps we do not know
What to expect.
If so, welcome

And we can all share surprises.

There will soon be a greeting and a scripture verse
Before the Sunday service starts.
Sunday, the first day of the week
Remembering Jesus, present with us now.

Confession

Sorry!
Did I tread on your toes?
I wasn't looking where I was going.
Negligence.

Sorry!
Did I hurt your feelings?
I couldn't help myself,
Speaking out of turn as I did.
I should have been able
To stop myself.
Weakness.

Sorry!
I was wrong
I decided not to help you
And now I am ashamed.
It was my own deliberate fault.
Confession.

The Word

How can we know?
How can we learn?
How can we tell the right from wrong?

How can we move
Without a guide
Or just decide

If we should go along
With all the others
In the crowd?

God spoke aloud
Through prophets, once upon a time.
And now, yes, it is so
He speaks today to you and me
In gentle whispers in our inmost ear.
We hear by seeing how some others live
And we can read
The words that have come down the years
In scripture.

The Creed

There was a time
One thousand and six hundred years ago
When scholars met
To write down what united
Christians from all over the known world.
Then. In the city of Nicea.

It is good to know
What happened in the past, to make a creed;
A 'credo'(Latin) meaning 'I believe'
And history is what we're making here
An act of faith, and will.
Faith for today, and a will to be obedient
For tomorrow and beyond.

Credo. I believe.

The Offertory Procession

Who are these people?
Why are they standing
Waiting to walk up the aisle to the altar?

They represent all of us, neighbours and family
They are the symbols, processing in place of us.
Two carry plates, awaiting our offerings.
What do you read on these pieces of paper?
A promise to make a payment to someone.
This is not silver- This is a symbol.

What else do they carry, these friends to God's table?
Bread to be broken and wine to be tasted.
A feast in a promise, foretaste of eternity.
Water for cleansing, the heart and the chalice
Remembrance in symbols, blood, body and baptism.
We, too, will soon come, each becoming an offering.
Sharing in Christ, offered once here for all of us.

Karaoke Christmas

It's going to be a Karaoke Christmas
Sing along with angels in the sky
Bring along your gifts with kings for Crisis
Sin's been a long time passing, wave goodbye.

May God be with you, Merry Christmas morning
Who will buy? It's beautiful and new
Every day's a gift, each date expiring
Every prayer has answers, now, in you.

Yours the offering, yours the life for living
Many need your joy, today new-born
Second helpings, generously giving
Share your love, with Christ, this holy morn.

Reunion

Heaven may be something like this
To stand at chancel steps and see the Peace
And hear and feel the Peace exchanged
Between saints who have not met for half

A lifetime. A celebration of an ending
With only a little sadness. An arriving, coming together
In love and joy of recognition through the
Wrinkles of the years, the marks of change
And growth because of pain and loss transformed.

There is emotion, each remembering the sharing
And the individual times
Of apprehension and the yielding of sharp edges
To the laser scalpel of the Spirit
And what came afterwards in many layers of memory.
But today a soul-felt happiness in each other
And a straightening of shoulders and a lifting
Of the eyes at the breaking of the Bread.

The Ballad Of Joe And Mary Church

It was out in the East where the legend
Had its origin, they say
On an isolated mountain where a holy man
Set up a place
To pray
And a hermitage appeared as if the
Spirit had established
Heaven's Bridge
Then the pilgrims started seeking out
God's word they heard from
Messiah's Ridge.

It was early in the morning when the pilgrims first
Knocked on the Church's door
To ask the way to go to find the holy man
With words for
Evermore
And the family just pointed up the
Hill at first and opened
Up the bridge
But then Joe and Mary Church set up

The signposts to
Messiah's Ridge.

Now Joe and Mary knew a prophecy
About their mountain-top
And they eagerly invited in the pilgrims
For a comfort
Stop
Then they shared their bread and water with the
Travellers stumbling on
Across the bridge
That was when Joe and Mary Church set up
The clearway to
Messiah's Ridge.

Once the path was cleared and straightened
Then a two-way highway soon led up and down
And there came a knock at midnight
From a figure in a
Hermit's gown.
'Will you let me in to see the people
This side of
The bridge?'
So now Joe and Mary host the
Incarnation from
Messiah's Ridge.

The star was out in the East where the journey
Had its origin, they say
To a multi-storey car-park with no privacy
The wise men came
To pray
Where the Incarnate One appeared as if the
Spirit had established
Heaven's Bridge
But we must now prepare the highway
For our God descending from
Messiah's Ridge.

The Emptying

You did not know icebergs at sea
But as God's Word you set
Absolute Zero and Freezing Point for me
When things came to be.

You did not walk on lava fields
But as God's Word you let
Earth's molten core and live volcanoes free
To bring new life to be.

You did not see
Glaciers or hot springs
Perhaps not Glastonbury
But you saw death for me.

Boy of the desert prayer
Knowing the silence and the voice.
Child of the Temple
Learning a creed.

Outcast from home
Sensing an Origin.
Prophet of siege
Longing to warn them.

You did not know our day.
Did you fore-see
This present time and many more
To be?

The Knife Edge

God is at the knife edge where things happen,
The hair-trigger between alternative universes
Is His to squeeze or release at His will.
But He also delegates and allows

Skeletal fingers seeking to abuse their power
To change the world into their image
By unleashing death before the allotted time.

On either side of many arguments
Quoting 'Crusade', 'Jihad', 'The Will of God'
They exercise control of others
And quite forget submission of the self.

Now is the time, yes, now, to pray
And beg before His throne to say the word
To whisper in the ear of vengeful men
(And women, too) of peace and self-restraint.

How can they fail to hear, who worship Him?
How can they close their ears to consequence?
How can we shout loudly enough to ensure
The whispering Spirit's voice takes up the strain?

The Night The Poetry Caught Fire

The Advent concert, candle-lit
With night-lights round the tall pulpit,
My voice projected six feet higher
And then the poetry caught fire.

Rehearsal went without a hitch,
The microphone was on full pitch;
The reading lamp with coils of wire
Presented no strong risk of fire

But when my turn came to recite
A poem about Christmas Night,
Like incense smoke was rising higher;
The night the poetry caught fire.

My concentration almost slipped
As flickering flames across the script

Spread from the corner held too near
The candle bringing Christmas cheer.

The brass quintet were quite amazed
As my first stanza gently blazed.
A ripple spread across the choir
The night the poetry caught fire.

The congregation had to smile,
God's sense of humour all the while
Had placed my pride upon the pyre,
The night my poetry caught fire.

The Perfect Day

We shall pass through the Refiner's fire
On that perfect Day
And God will share His deep desire
To shape us in His way.
Unfailing love as never known
In life before we reached His throne
So we will be no more alone
In that eternal Day.

His angels will be at our side
That perfect Advent Day.
They exist His actions to describe
And call, 'Up and away!'
A following breeze and a steady course
Relationships without remorse
For better but no longer worse
On that healing Day.

Our work will satisfy our hearts
In the morning of that Day.
Completion before Sabbath starts
For family we pray
May we with them your Kingdom know

And joyfully chatter as we go
For time is short, may hours be slow
Together towards that Day.

On Earth we build a concrete path
To lead us to that Day
Our grandchildren, the aftermath
May never tread this way
The choice is clear, He must return
Their names we will in Heaven learn
Through each perplexity discern
His will for all, that Day.

Saint Michael will forever sing
Sonnets of praise, that Day
And works of art God's people bring
As they create and say
Communion, Compline, joyful psalms
To laugh, embrace with open arms
And celebrate while music charms
The beauty of that Day.

Contentment and His presence now
Before that perfect Day
Can be achieved as this, His vow
Will never pass away.
Beneath the stars His peace we see
Our map is open on our knee
Across the world we'll fly to be
At journey's end, that Day.

The Personal Rainbow

The rainbow's arc is a covenant sign
A promise of safety to come
But side by side as we view that hope
The sign is a private one.
For the sun decrees that your shadow points

To the highest place on the bow.
The apex there is for you alone
And you and you and you.
The raindrops mirror the spectrum light
In an individual way
And the perfect arc brings the perfect sight
Of a personal covenant day.

Without Christmas

Without Christmas I would not have led this life
Without Christ, no Christmas, grandchildren or wife.
No midnight mass, no glimpse of the divine,
No witnessing the consecrated wine
Being gratefully received.

Without Christmas there would be no hope or joy
Based on the birth of this eternal boy.
No babe of Bethlehem, no manger sign
No star leading the world to Palestine
No God incredibly conceived.

Without Christmas where would we have come to be?
Worshipping with Pan-pipes round a Yuletide tree?
No gifts reminding of salvation's plan
No Heavenly Father reaching out to man
Yearning to be believed.

Chapter 3

A Heart For Mission

Foreword

In this volume we meet a rare combination: in Christopher dwell both the hymn-writer and the mystic visionary, one who walks faithfully within an earthed and grounded tradition while at the same time flying beyond its limits to help us glimpse the stars.

A master of paradox, he takes us to the place where the blueprint of God's love and power is traced indelibly across the shifting sands of human history. He draws us more deeply into a reality where 'the architect is the design, the river is the source and the light is the way.' He invites us, as we watch an aircraft soaring over London, beneath the dimming disc of a dawn moon, to allow that same moon to reflect back to us the very different conditions of life prevailing at the flight's destination. He brings the throb of the world's affairs into the timeless stillness of a suburban church, where a sundial measures slowly the frantic passing moments of a deepening international crisis, held by a few, in silent prayer.

Christopher's poetic heart is a treasure store of epiphany moments, where, for example, the fleeting image of a yellow kite evokes the essence of a grieved-for father's lifetime. We find ourselves in the place beyond place where the unspoken can be embraced, the nearly-but-not-quite can be encountered, and the prayer that lodges somewhere between our heart and our lips can be recognised in an image that lies deeper than words.

Thank you, Christopher, for sharing some of your epiphanies, so that we might discover our own, and recognise afresh the stirrings of God within us and amidst our everyday experience.

Margaret Silf May 2006

A Heart For Mission - Metre 8 7. 8 7. D Trochaic

Give us, Lord, a heart for Mission;
May we serve you where we are;
May we speak your words and listen,
Always guided by your star;
May we share our inspiration,
Tell the world the truth we learn,
Build together sure foundations,
Working and praying for your return.

Give us, Lord, a heart for sharing
All the blessings that we see;
For each other joyfully caring
Praise in all we try to be;
Turn our vision into living
Where we are and where we go,
Celebrate your call and giving
All our hearts our Lord to know.

A Hill Of Beans For Peace

The Imam prayed in the Catholic church for peace
His black cap on his head showing respect.
Allah the Merciful was called upon in prayer
Surrounded by the stations of the Cross.

Salvation Army Captains, priests and lay
Men and women ordained to serve the Lord
United by the call to prayer that day
Sang fervently against the threat of war.

The symbol of their unity and faith
Was hollow only in the visual aid
An empty box with windows spelling 'Peace'
Placed by the pulpit waiting for the throng.

The invited queues soon formed to make a vow

To action following on from faithful prayer
And contributed a shovelful of beans
Just beans, ordinary, comical like us
Amounting to the promised strength from God
A hill of beans, a parting cup of tea, and Thou
Hast heard us, will we overcome, some day?

And A Middleton New Year

St. John the Baptist's bells ring clear
Boldly announcing this New Year
And with their penultimate chime
We try to translate Auld Lang Syne.

Two oh oh two, this palindrome
Could find no more appreciative home
Than in the Rectory, warm and large,
Where son-in-law is priest-in-charge.

The Staffordshire horizon; bright
Brief fireworks dimly mimic light
Three-quartering Moon and vivid stars
Reflect or generate as theirs.

The grandchildren are good as gold
We baby sit, our Lang quite Auld
In New Year sixty-four or three.
Some red for you, some white for me
Our glasses clink. Then we retire
With backward glance at embering fire.

Before The Diagnosis

I don't know what's to come
But I do know that you're there.
I was curled up in your presence
Comfortable, sustained by prayer
On the operating table,

In your smiling peace at rest,
While the surgeon gave the injection
To perform the scheduled test.

In this morning's Bible reading
Stephen saw you standing there,
At your Father's right hand, greeting
Welcoming, answering his prayer.

Blueprint In The Sand

In responding to the random
God is constantly creating;
In response to wise men's questions asking, 'Why?'
 'Why this present, why that past
And why the future that is waiting?'
Here His answer is transparent:
 'Here am I'

I am asking for the meaning
Of this galaxy eternal;
I am seeking the coincidental plan
To be spread out here before me
In my quest for the diurnal
Game of chance to be explained
In terms of man.

For the ordinary stuff of life
Is where Time's wheel tangential
Touches, here and now, the moment that we share
And the concrete of this pavement
And the wood beneath my pencil
Where the paper meets the table
Must be there.

For the pre-existing will that needs
Imperative obedience
Is at once the loving, flexible response

To the gift of free expression
And free will and of convenience
Constant change to be expected
Human wants.

Explanations in the rigid
Language of exclusive dogmas
Cannot yet embrace realities we see.
There is 'both' and there is 'and',
There is 'spontaneous' and 'planned',
There is a blueprint in the sand
Awaiting me.

Day One

An aircraft flies beneath
The large but waning early morning moon,
Not quite the 'E.T.' cliché but an image
In frosty springtime London, free from sandstorms.
Distant desert skies mirror this sight,
The same shaped moon, her ancient craters
Pock-marking another desert, another dawn
Another world, again.

Could this sphere but reflect to us the eyes
In those far sandy faces lifted up
To search the skies for threat or hope,
Or weather forecast for their flight,
She would forge links of empathy
Between praying human beings this dawning day.

Dear Colleague

What is it like to be surrounded by fanatics?
Followers of what to you may seem to be
A long dead prophet
People whose life decisions are made
In the light of his guidance?

What is it like to see this sickening 'goodness'?
Almost tee-total, never smoking, hardly swearing, seeming pacifists
Who recycle their cardboard
And require you to save all envelopes
Driven by an invisible, spooky compulsion?

What is it like to work among the trappings
Of a religion that makes little sense to you?
But step inside, love.
See the struggle, hear the unspoken anger
Share the early morning tears.

We are here because we know our limitations.
We are committed because we remember our failures.
There was once a time of total abandonment
In response to an overwhelming sense of emptiness
And a hand reaching through time to ruffle our hair.

From Galilee To Here

As Jesus broke the loaves they brought
Eyes raised to God in prayer
Barley became a sacrament
From many fields to there.

As Jesus, taking pickled fish
Encouraged all to share
Salt, miracles for all the Earth
Began to spread from there.

As Jesus takes each one of us
Leading to here from there
He smiles to bless our pilgrim steps
From Galilee to here.

Hold That Word

Hold that word
That almost escaped,
Pursue the echo.

Hold that place
Where words have failed
On the tip of your tongue.

Hold that thought
Of almost inspiration,
Where emptiness intrudes.

Hold that poem
At the moment of waking,
Before the white-wash of day.

Hold that prayer
Suspended over the world,
And feel Him speak.

God, Forsaken (A Meditation On Psalm 22)

Lord Jesus, you memorised this psalm.
Did it speak to you on walks in the desert
Or on the flat roof in Nazareth as the
Night wind blew, cool upon your face?

The words were on your lips as you died.
We take comfort from your forsaken-ness
As we, too, can know loneliness and can sense
Abandonment by God.

You truly walked where we walk
But the psalm has an end
As well as a beginning.

Did you shrink from the prophetic details
Of your crucifixion, clearly spoken?
Yet did you take heart from David's vision
Of your future time?

The poet king's prophecy, through the Holy Spirit
Of the nations' worship
And all families of the world loving you?
Through your word, your wisdom
Your sacrifice, your loneliness, your death
Your resurrection?

The preaching yet to come
Your gospel turning the world upside-down
All peoples learning of your life
And death and uncompromising love?

Did you rejoice in youth and remember
As you died that this would rend the veil
And open the narrow path to God?

Did you know, as you died, did you know?

Hopton Wafers Churchyard

I stood by the yew tree remembering the future
Witnessing families over the years
Where the sounds of the playground once echoed the music
The sight of us loving, embracing through tears.

By the bench for the milkman the path's third right turning
Carried in front of me walking in pairs
Numbers unknowable, memories in mourning
Dear ones, unborn ones, each shouldering their cares.

The bearers with dignity labour together
The circle is forming, the precious load rests
Suddenly sunshine breaks through cloudy weather

The coffin is warmed and the blessings are blessed.

What goes around comes around this sheltered corner
Wild flowers and birdsong, the bridge and the stream
The hill to the farmhouse, the Shropshire bees' murmur
The background to living, the birth of the dream.

This church knew God's presence, the twentieth century
Holy Communions, thanks-givings for birth
The family singing and serving in sanctuary
Baptisms, offering fruits of the Earth.

I go away comforted, tributes are tidied
The stone reassessed by the neighbouring space
I shall return, after time reunited
Where the wedding bells rang will be my starting place.

How Was Your Day?

Search me and tell me, Father, tonight, you lived it with me.
In your presence I gave praise at sunrise.
 'Thank you for bringing us safely', I said
 'To the beginning of this day', and meant it.

I prayed for my loved ones each in turn and I do so again.
I commit my soul, my wife's soul and them all to you this night
For cleansing from sin, filling with your Holy Spirit
And protection with the Blood of Jesus.
May we come to a living faith in you through Him
And may our faith be strengthened.

Thank you for these; and the credits roll
As name after name is mentioned before you
All present and correct this blessed night.
This morning the call to prayer and to prepare
Led half way through the Christmas card familiar list.
Tomorrow maybe all will be remembered
And I pray with thanks for those who will remember me.

Together we are stronger, I with them and you
And they with me.
We share this bond of love, this fellowship uniting us beyond
Tomorrow and the unknown days to come
When we approach your closer presence.
As the Comforter inspires us to believe, I leave this safe with you.
I still feel close to those who went ahead
The communion of saints and sinners too
Entirely dependent on your grace.

Forgive me for my many sins, and bless us as we sleep
In Jesus' Holy name.
Amen.

Iran Morning

As the crow flies, straight to the Cypress tree
So speeds my soul, dear Lord, to Thee.

Where the painted mountain meets the painted sky
I'll seek my God until I die.

My eyes will rise up to the hill
The source of strength is with me still.

The traffic's roar, the donkey's plod
The journey, fast or slow, to God.

A single orange on the tree
A symbol, Lord, of trust in Thee.

This orange, donkey, hill and crow
Like God, will never let me go.

Lord, Teach Us To Pray - Metre 13 10 13 10

Lord, teach us to pray as you prayed in the wilderness
Show us your presence in silence and song

From Temple and mountain-top lead us to holiness
Tempted and tried, Lord, help us to be strong.

Teach us to love as you share our humanity
Turning to words that your Spirit inspired
Trusted and true they reveal your divinity
Leading to Heaven through cloud and through fire.

Teach us to worship in work-place and sanctuary
Learning and loving and serving our Lord
In our life of faith may we spend each day prayerfully
Placing ourselves in the Presence of God.

Michaelmas

The Archangel draws his sword across the sky
And legions follow in response to prayer.
Their wings translate them into octaves high
Beyond the ultimate reaches of the human ear,
Where sheep-dogs answering to the circling sound
Will lift their heads beyond their master's voice
To seek the autumnal message all around,
And find confusion in their new-found choice.

But we can only see the trembling green
Of leaves about to turn to darker hues,
Surmise the reason for the breeze unseen,
Redoubling intercession at the news
From far away where miracles are born,
And learn how God has spared His Galveston.

29 September 2005 Footnote:
One week previously, Hurricane Rita was reported to be heading straight for Galveston. A church group in London, undoubtedly among many others, prayed specifically for the area. By 25 September Rita had changed direction. Damage was much less than predicted. Were these two historical events related?

Palms Of Jericho

Perhaps they brought from Jericho
The palms they threw beneath the hooves.
Perhaps they waved them up the road
The pilgrims bound for Zion.

Perhaps they watched Him lead the way
Disciples full of fear and awe,
'Let us go and die with Him
And cast our cloaks before Him'.

Perhaps we, too, should trophies bring
And leave behind the city of palms
To reach the gates, 'Hosanna' cry
And follow as the echoes die.

Paradox

Welcome to the kingdom
Where poor are blessed,
Where last are first,
Where death can be victory,
Where separation brings closeness.

Welcome to the garden
Where lamb and lion wander,
Where mist brings fruit,
Where days grow cool
His voice is heard.

Welcome to the city
Where the architect is the design,
Where the leaves of the avenue are for healing,
Where the river is the source,
Where the light is the way.

Prayer Tank

Sunbeam watching, sundial slow, within a weekday church
Where two or three have gathered God is here.
From Harvest-time to Advent our Creator and our Judge,
Our King, our Prince and Spirit welcome prayer.
International developments have brought us to our knees;
According to His promises He hears our puzzled pleas
As the experts are deliberating far across the seas
Like St. Peter we are trusted with the North Door keys.

By taking thought we cannot reach conclusions;
The world is full of clamour and despair.
All we can do is bring Him our confusions
And trust that at each bedside He'll be there.
The crisis internationally deepens with each hour;
In the stained glass Eastern window Jesus holds the orb with power.

Stay Close

I don't know how it works, Lord, but I'm here with a petition
I don't know how it works, Lord, but I'm here to make a prayer
For a loved one with a problem, for a friend in bad condition
For a soldier who is dying, please be there.

I don't know if you hear me when I'm pouring out my heart, Lord
I don't know if your Heaven reaches here
But I'm here to take a gamble that I really cannot lose
And I'm ready to take action, please be near.

Will you hear the prayer I offer, if it really is a prayer?
I believe, please help my trembling unbelief
Will you give the strength I need, Lord,
Give me faith where faith falls short?
Stay close by me, do not leave me in my grief.

Taking The Oath

Lord, we can be your witnesses.
We have seen the altar linen purity
At morning Communion embrace the stained glass blue
In readiness for the memorial of your life.

Lord, we can be your witnesses.
We have heard the church clock in the winter fields
Telling the half hours towards a glad new year
With blessings in the family, gifts from you.

Lord, we can be your witnesses.
The harvest smell of apples by the font
Reminding of the early years with you
Sometimes unheeding, sometimes overwhelmed.

Lord, we can be your witnesses.
The taste of quenching candle smoke and spare wine
Consumed before the congregation leaves
In reverence trying to recall the Host.

Lord, we must be your witnesses.
The Christmas holly prickles warn of care
To take when reaching others in your name
Not to recoil when witness is rebuffed.

Lord, do you need our witness?
Our senses speak to us of things beyond
You call us all to worship at your birth
And we will take the oath and speak for you.

To See More Clearly

I took my place in the garden of my memories
Where the family played and talked
And laughed together as before.

There were picnics again, and games.
For the moment nobody had fallen over
And the sun was shining on the trees.

I took my seat as bidden by the prayer leader
Somewhere to feel secure, and find
That God was present to me
And I to Him
In this hour of stillness
As a psalm was read.

You were all around, remembered in love
As God's unfailing compassion was recalled;
For I knew in the depths of my silent spirit
That this had been my privilege and joy
To see the Father's smile
In the eyes of loved ones, family and friends,
True soul-companions sharing Heaven's news

The good news that wherever God is found
In this imperfect, waiting, familiar world
Promising Paradise hints of things to come
Have taken form between us in the touch
Of hands, and voices heard encouraging
To be the best we can, that we are close
Together and to Him.

Thou art in Heaven, we hear; where Heaven is known
Thou art, Our Father, day by day more clear.

Twelve Epiphanies

What do the angels say to you today?
What do the angels say?

Beside the still waters
Under the fig tree
In the shade of the vine

He has been here
He is here
He is coming again.

In the sand-fall around the desert footprint
By the mark of the writing finger on the dusty pavement
In the dry riverbed where the reptile still lies in wait
He passed this way
His message remains here
He will bring the living water.

Where the valley echoes to the bells around the necks of sheep
and goats together
Where the sweat, like blood, congeals on the fallen olive leaves
Where the rough splinters score skin from the slumping back
He will choose with justice
He accepted suffering here
He will die today.

What do the angels say to you today?
What do the angels say?

Where the cold stone will never be warmed by another body
Where the bread crumbs and embers mingle on the beach
Where the clouds part in joyful welcoming
He has no final resting place here
He has completed the breakfast of healing

He is with us once again.

Yellow

It was a yellow kite,
A box-kite that he flew
On a gentle, rolling hill.

If I tried hard, I might
Still hear his voice, a few

Kind words my memory fill.

Awake, before the night
Falls, I remember you,
My Dad…and always will.

Chapter 4

Taking The Minutes

A Hard Debating We Had Of It…
(with acknowledgements to T.S. Eliot)

…At one point in the journey even intolerance
Was ruled intolerable.
And many voices echoed the call to prayer.
The pilgrimage was slow
But every camel's foot-print closely scrutinised
Looked at from all angles and reluctantly
Left behind. Yet we would not have missed this travelling
Led by a star from the East and the centre of out-reaching.

The revelation to our tribe was most particular
While the prophecy could be described as general
In its generosity, but whence came its source?
The single sun was misty in a far off land
But closer to the kingdom of our search
There was a shining undiminished.

Five times daily there was prayer.
On the way there were stops for food
And [Dare it be said?] wine after sunset
And hospitable sharing of our gifts and alms.
All hearts were gladdened by the Eastern spices
And rich Oriental flavours to the meat, ritually clean.

In the end we reached new understanding
Of the brothers and sisters in their sandy caravanserai
But did we really comprehend
Each other?

A Globe Theatre

If Bard but knew
The Earth so blue
From horn-ed crater seen
Behind gloved thumb
So dear become
What sonnets would have been!

The sisters seven
Medieval Heaven
Displayed for men's delight.
Had eye so keen
This blessed been
What praise would grace their night!

Beyond the air
The visions there
Expand both time and space.
Did sainted Hubble
By toil and trouble
Suspend belief and faith?

From dust to dust
Elemental rust
Formed diamond, pen and blood.
Exploding stars
Made prison bars
From such primordial mud.

The snowball trail
Forms comet tail
Blown outward from the Sun.
Had Will thus read
This portent dread
What poetry had begun!

Dining Room Three
(With acknowledgements to Rupert Brooke)

When you were there, and you, and you
Moments of faith were shared, I too
Remembering and laughing, one of all
Recalled the enfolding Spirit fall
On youth and pensioner, setting free
Our souls and bodies; they and we
Brought all the inspiring moments by
With jest and sadness. Memory's eye
Saw Easter joy grow happier yet.
With unfailing love, God cancelled debt.
The Holy Spirit, Breath and Flame
And Light of Christ, to Earth you came.

Oh, Trinity, we saw you true,
When you were there, and you, and you.

Genesis 3 In Lent

What are the questions which this story answers?
Who wrote it down, this poem of truth and wrongs?
What was his purpose, what his inspiration?
When giving form to centuries of songs?

Why is there pain and why do people suffer?
Why are we lost, beneath this moon and sun?
We see the beauty but in all creation
Who heard the Lord who spoke and knew that it was done?

'In the beginning, God', is how he started
Where else would be this desert father's source?
Through all his years of mystic contemplation
And trying to see the wisdom through the wars.

This Hebrew script became the base of Scripture,
These thoughts that shine through these iconic lines

Contain the guidance, faith and understanding
We need to hear God's word that leads us to the skies.

Global Mourning : A Microcosmic Event

Tonight, considering global warming,
Pessimistic thoughts are forming.
Is joy coming in the morning?
Why not pray to God above?

Should we found another planet?
Build an Eden Star, and man it?
Carbon is the problem-Ban it!
Endorse the element of Love.

We discuss predictions gloomy
Our manoeuvres are not so roomy
A new idea is coming to me
What happened to 'In God We Trust'?

Can we trust the United Nations
When most ignore recommendations
Reducing coal, oil, conflagrations
Ashes to ash and dust to rust?

Shall we rely on the Second Coming?
Will the humming-birds still be humming,
The carbon drums of war keep drumming,
Or Hydrogen fuel keep us alive?

Should our fate not be distinct now
Or like dinosaurs be extinct now?
Return to reason and instinct now
With God's help we will survive.

Coda
The world's agenda reached congestion
Did not hear every man's suggestion

Powerful voices begged the question
And no action plan arrived.

Home Grown Toast

Let us drink to Hugh's home-grown tomatoes
He has never home-grown them before.
He has little idea of the colour or shape
Or the height they will grow to beside his backdoor
Or God's plan for his home-grown tomatoes.

Let us drink to this evening together
We have not had this evening before.
We have little idea of how it will go.
Or the colour and shape of the Church we will know.
Or the depth of our fellowship, the future in store…
Here's to God's plan for our evening together.

And now Hugh has toasted tomatoes.

Intelligent Design

Ideas collide within my head and spin
Off random moons from Mars and Proto Earth.
They coalesce and within weeks have formed
The beauty of the future Queen of Nights,
Which was not my intention. Thus says God?
It happens when we try to concentrate
On the big picture language goes astray
And unintended consequences rise
If one abandons one's omnipotence
And takes one's eyes off gravity and the ball.

In the beginning was the Word who started
Information and a plan, all there
At first, the end from the beginning clear
And indestructible, how would it be
And end and unfold and now be revealed?

On looking back it is quite obvious
For everything to be just as it is
It all just had to happen as it did.
But looking forward from each vantage point
On taking breath and stock and time to think
When in the process inextricably
Involved in living can we have a choice?

The days like sliced bread stretch into the past
The best thing since philosophy began
For understanding time and consequence.
Perhaps the infinite loaf begins to curl
And writhe within the fabric of space time
And fold back on itself, a tangled string
The plaything of some mad celestial cat.

Or does it march straight on beyond the screen
Like solid credits opening 'Star Wars'
Perspective leading forward into where?

So in all this where is the prophet voice?
The Hebrew poet spinning his own yarn
Not mad but inspired by the desert air
By silence and the overwhelming stars
Which must not be themselves the source of all
But share with us a common origin
Not chance but by intelligent design.

Just Another Day In The Wilderness

Good morning, sheep.
Jethro sends his regards.
What excitement awaits us today?
A spot of munching, perhaps?
Maybe a brush with a mountain lion or two?
There's a parched river- bed to wander into
If young Ben-Larry feels like an adventure.
One day I'll hatch some plans for you, my lads

Especially the ones without blemish.

Eighty years old and this is it.
There might be another forty to go.
Looking back on my mid-life crisis
Why did I lose my temper with that Egyptian?
I could have been like Father Joseph
And ruled over all Egypt.

I was brought up near the throne.
My early training and experience are wasted here.
Zippy-baby and the boys are great
But where is the ambition of my youth?
I have even lost confidence in my hieroglyphics.

Nothing ever happens in this job.
The desert is as dry as tinder.
Someone has even set fire to that bush over there.
Now that could really start some problems…

Lord, Draw Near…

…as we stand at the door and knock
 With our oxygen dependency
 Grant us the Breath of Life

…as we approach with our oblations
And libations and green creations
May we share in the Grace
Said and received,
Quite undeserved

…as we experience our minutes and our moments
In our laughter at the ridiculous
In our amazement at the sublime
May we see you more clearly
With first-century, eyewitness eyes

…as we recall your image, painted, waiting,
The Light of the World
May we have the courage to open and welcome
And let you change our lives

…as we heed the altar call
On cathode ray tube
Or overhead projector

…as we see golden visions
And take our place to stand among the nine candlesticks

…as we become one in the Spirit
In the shadow of the Most High,
This night and every night…

Lord, draw near.

Pitter-Patter Noster

The sound of tiny feet
The whisper of the liturgy
The tapping to the beat

Listening together
In collaborative prayer
The silence of Community
The Trinity is there.

5000 hermits jostling
Strap-hanging sacred space
The Mendicant Evangelists
Seek the means of grace.

Theophilus is edified
By desert contemplation
Abba, Father, let me be
Enriched by an oration.

Crucible monasticism
River banks of faith
Where flow our gospel values
A committed, stable base.

The Jerusalem Community
In a city where they brought
The insights of the desert
An encounter with the Lord.

The fire of St. Anthony
Is still alight today
With Anglican Franciscans
And Benedict Rules OK.

Max's Tale

The Animal Service at old St. Chad's
Is being held this New Year's Day
And here I am in the car park
At the 'Cock Inn', so they say.
Four hundred legs are milling around
Humans and dogs, so far
But what are those five Alsatians
Doing so close to my car?

The horses have set off at quite a pace
I'm straining hard to see
My friend the Greyhound is trotting along
So proud of her pedigree.
This isn't a race to the finish
As the Yorkies and Boxer showed
But why did Lady Doberman
Walk on my stretch of road?
I've settled down in the choir stalls
The church is like an Ark.
The Reverend prayed for us animals
And we gave the occasional bark.

I'm sharing my bowl of water
Now we're out in the yard again
But why did that young Dalmatian
Look at me like that then?

We've all had photographs taken now
Though we didn't exactly pose.
The ponies have left the footpath
In need of the garden hose.
There's word of bacon sandwiches
And mulled wine along the way
For the Animal Service at old St. Chad's
Has been held this New Year's Day.

Social Climbing

What is on the Agenda?
What is to be done?
We've laughed until we're tender
We're having so much fun
This year will be a triumph
For incorrigible lives
And one of our chaps is married
To one of the Blackheath Wives.

We might invite a Bishop
We gather there's somebody new.
There ought to be lively discussions
Led by one of the crew.
I suppose we'll hear from the Rector
How perfection reigns and survives
But one of our chaps is married
To one of the Blackheath Wives.

Let's have a report on ageing
By one who hasn't yet
Or a driving police instructor
On when to turn on the jet.

We'll tell the Old Grim Reaper
Whenever he arrives
That one of our chaps is married
To one of the Blackheath Wives.

The Cry On The Street

Who will buy alternative worship?
Me oh my! How great it will be
Flying high with overhead visions
With truth that will not die
And words that never lie
Post-modernism who will buy?

For when the vicar has no sermon
And there are songs that sound so new
From multi-media we'll be learnin'
Until we know just what to do…

Who will buy the Gospel of Jesus?
Multi-task wherever you see
Satisfy your deepest desire
Religion in a box for me.

The Dashing 'Why Start?' Rant

Now you take your partners, one, two, three
The cat's in the bag, so he won't see me.
Your programme notes are in your hand
You can sort your anger if you understand
What are your priorities
My respect is better than his.

You can hit your head on the cupboard door
Give a beautiful smile and ask for more.
Swing to the left, swing to the right
'Til Tony Blair is out of sight.
If your soul is fettered to an office stool

You can still survive with the Golden Rule
Forgiveness better start at home
With the toothpaste cap, you're on your own.

Inanimate objects all in a row
Lining up to make you go
'Bother!' and 'Dear me!', grumpy old men
Dust yourself down and start again.
Give a soft answer, not what you meant
Choose a word like 'Excellent!'

The Kidbrooke Beatitudes

Blessed are the individuals who are converted
They shall grow into a like-minded congregation.
Blessed are the members of the Body of Christ
They shall not be democratically elected.

Blessed are the incumbents in the parish system
They shall receive the cure of souls.
Blessed are the new ways of being church
They shall lead to worship in the fellowship of Saint Cyber-space.

Blessed are those who shall preserve Christian Distinctiveness
They shall experience the reality of their baptism.
Blessed are those who work with other faiths
They shall enter into deeper understanding of their own.

Blessed is the Christianising of institutions
It shall give new meaning to the Kingdom of Heaven.
Blessed are the individuals who are Christianised
They shall see with their own eyes the coming of the Lord.

Blessed are you when you are closely questioned
Rejoice and be glad because great is the illumination
For in the same way the elders questioned the Lord
And marvelled at his answers in the Temple.

The Padre

We saw duty in the eye of the beholder,
Heard the poetry of a Falkland Isle return,
Learned the motives of a Pastor to the soldier,
Felt the passion of a long vocation burn.

The Verse

A chieftain King received this verse in ecstasy.
His courtier memorised the Hebrew sounds for worship.
A prophet told forth the message against a tyrant.
His servant scratched it on a piece of clay.

The Baptist's forebears used it to incite rebellion.
Jesus made it perfectly his own in Aramaic
And a generation believed.

An evangelist dictated it in Greek.
A scribe immortalised it in papyrus scrolls.
Some martyrs soon defended it to the death.
Slaves died in the arena singing it in triumph.
An emperor discovered it with his mother.

A desert mystic meditated on it for a month.
Hierarchies of priests expounded on it as their text.
An Irish monk decorated it with leaves.
Byzantium set it in a splendid ceiling.
Francis was said to
Have preached it to the birds.

Conquerors carried it, rulers endorsed it.
Bishops concealed it from their flock.
Until printers disseminated it in the vernacular.
Shakespeare quoted it, heretics burned for it.
Missionaries carried it, translated it, lived it.
From all our nations some embraced it.
Unknown millions

Have learned it in their own tongue.
Reawakenings have aroused it.

At the end of its third millennium
Chieftain Kings receive it in ecstasy.

The Very Idea

Edwardian London, a horse-drawn pantechnicon
Piled high with tea chests, my grandfather's brainwave.
Came down from Lancashire seeking his fortune
Pavements of Walthamstow, tea dust not gold dust.

Blue Anchor Yard railway arches were stables
Just North of the Tower Bridge, still a great wonder.
Drivers and coopers recycled the tea chests
Out with the lining, bent nails to be hammered in.

Filtered of splinters, tea for the family
Taken in houses of increasing opulence
Moved from the East End to leafier Chingford
Home for nine children, close to the forest.

Turn again, Thomas, your profit from cubism
Purveyor of tea chests to importing tradesmen
Shrewd, kindly Methodist, pillar of chapel
Eldest son lost eleven weeks before Armistice.

Bowler hat portrait with silvery moustache
Stands on his chiffonier by green china art pot
These my inheritance from his idea
[With Mother's advantage of good education].

To The Ed.

Sir,

Does God care how we fare

When we wage war?
What is war for?
Is it oil?
Or faith on the boil?
Do we lance
While we have the chance?
Is it food?
Or clean air that is good?
Bad men's plans in the sands
Of time?
While we still
Have time to write
We will.

Yours

Men who meet at St James'
For Church.

We Three

Quite small for a club
Three men in a pub
Their cup contained knowledge so rare
I can tell in a minute
How much there was in it
While admitting I couldn't be there.

Chapter 5

Family And Other Blessings

February The Fourteenth, 2001

'To Paddy, with love of Valentine's Day,'
My pen slipped on your card.
We shared a gentle smile at this,
Perhaps you found it hard.

For is my love 'of Valentine'
Or is it love for you?
Am I in love with love's idea
Or love's ideal in you?

'Or even on,' my pen decided
Then to make amends,
Inserting before 'Valentine's',
Hoping we would be friends.

For is my love appropriate
For this stage in our life?
The gentle smile shares partnership
My Thirty-eight Valentine wife.

A Sunny Hillside In Brentwood

The roses will be dead on the grave
But the memory lives anew
Of the afternoons when we gave
Our happy remembrance of you.

A year since you opened your eyes,
I wonder what you saw,
In that moment we shared your demise
And would hear your voice no more.

That voice, with a careless smile,
Had made your wishes known
Where your sisters had rested a while
Was the place to make your own.

Your ashes to be interred
Or scattered on the ground
Where your sisters had preferred
To be buried, where we found

Three headstones bearing words
Of kindness and of loss
For three who had gone before
Each widow, with her spouse.

Each one the second wife
Of the man she lay beside,
In Brentwood's distant life
We'd grieved when six had died.

As a young man, shaking the hand
Of uncles now long gone,
I saw you understand,
You, too, had lost someone.

So lately we have returned
To the scene of forty years,
Successive groups who mourned
Supporting each other's tears.

A year since your turn came,
The chapel on the hill
In Brentwood looked the same
In sunshine we stood still.

Still, motionless the day,
Like all those days before
Together, come to pray,

A family once more.

My daughters, cousins, wife,
With words serene and strong
Remembering your life
With joyfulness and song,

And how these children small
Their Grandma loved to see
Going scampering down her hall;
Their strength now comforts me.

Autumn Song For Ciara

Have you noticed how the autumn trees
Are taking it in turns
To shed their leaves? The cherry bright
(I wonder how it learns)

Has been the first this year to spread
The table of the lawn
With cloth of golden, pointed shapes.
The damson next is shorn

Of later leaves where recently
The feast of fruit was set
Before the blackbirds and the fox
Not quite completed yet.

The apple is already bare
The cob-nuts shelter still.
Ash leaves hide the squirrel grey
While he eats his fill.

Our little beech, almost a hedge,
Is holding firmly on
To brown and crackling foliage
Until the New Year dawns

When green shoots elbow the leaves aside
To whisper on the earth
The sound that welcomes next year's song
As Spring will come to birth.

Best Friends And Brothers

Best friends and brothers
Freckled four- and six-years old
Walking home in harmony from school
Sharing their Grand- Dad's stripy, blue umbrella;
Johnny, tenderly protective of his charge,
Sheltering him from the early Autumn rain;
Lukey, confidently pointing out
The best places to cross the road.

We had the blessing of being present
At both these births
And now our busy programme in retirement
Joyfully includes these precious, routine days:
Memories in the making for future
Family legends.

Blue Crocuses

My father was always glad to see another Spring.
This is the thirty-second since he died.
He would have enjoyed strolling
In the garden of our house, the house he never knew
And discussing how the blue
Crocuses are always first to disappear
As if eaten by some living thing, still near
Pigeon or squirrel, quick to steal and hide.

My father was a dreamer but he loved the things of Earth.
A city dweller lately but a countryman by birth.
He photographed his son, aged four,
Beneath Welsh apple blossom in the War,

And flew my yellow kite one windy day
Breathless on rolling hills near Colwyn Bay.

Bryn

Come on, Bryn!
Come on out to play!
There's a world waiting for you.
There are mountains to climb,
Poems to write,
Songs to sing;
People to meet.

You already know your Mum & Dad.
You have heard their love
In their voices,
Their caresses,
Their warm embrace.
They are longing to meet you.

It is time for you to know
The other voices,
Family, friends, well-wishers.
You are so loved already
By so many.

Welcome, Bryn.
Here you are.
And your beauty and your strength
Surpass our dreams.

Coliemore Harbour

The eels were biting at Coliemore
In the early Pentecost sun
And Roshi, Lulu and Lukey
Took turns with the rod, one by one.

The cormorants dived in the Harbour
For their breakfast, more fishy than ours,
While Jodi, Becky and Ciara
Practised casting for almost two hours.

David was really the expert,
Posed for photographs with great aplomb
He had hooked a large piece of seaweed,
Plus his trousers and Jodi's left thumb.

Grand-Dad and Nanna ate croissants
In their directorial chairs
Ils n'y ont point de poissons
Quelques Brioches et Danish were theirs.

The eel Lulu caught (She was screaming)
Wriggled gratefully back to the sea.
It's quite one thing to cheer when you catch one
Conservation's marine biol'gy.

If you really must fly back to England
Then a pier is the place to depart
So Jodi and Lukey had breakfast,
Packed their bags, cheerful smiles, heavy hearts.

We had welcomed this Whit Sunday morning
With appropriate thoughts of new birth.
You are closer to God when you're fishing
Than anywhere else on His Earth.

Crowberry Lane

Yesterday I walked here as I waited
For the bus to bring the cheerful
Grandchildren from school.
Behind the farrier's [conveniently placed
For many paddocks of horses]
There was wood-smoke in the early Autumn air.

At the ford the mud was printed by his work
Where the thirsty animals had been allowed to drink
Arresting to a dawdling town-dweller's eye.
This was one feature even absent from
The wilder corners of my distant London garden.

Further on the hedgerows were a glorious profusion
Of orange rose hips turning scarlet
Among the pastel ivy greens
Red holly, black-thorn and deadly nightshade
Curling, yellow honeysuckle, elder and black-berries
Which were dying on the branch for lack of local interest.

All of these grow happily South of the Thames around my fences
But more and yet more flourish here
Unknown to me by name
The ideal beauty we aspire towards
In our church window Harvest decorations.

Behind the uncultivated hops down Vicarage Hill
The stubbled field extended beneath a haze of secondary green.
Today, returning in the sunshine, all is ploughed
Deep, rich brown furrows to the very edge
Where tufts of weeds had shared their short-lived prime
With a sapling ash which lies prostrate
Rebellion ended by the march of the turning year.

Dylan

What a day, Dylan!
What a happy day for your own
Inauguration! It augurs well,
A day when Joy came to the Hope Valley
And Hope came to the world,
The world to which we welcome you
With so much love.

Your brother, Bryn, was there.

Did you see him, with your Mum and Dad
Shining in your amazing, wide-open eyes?
Did you see the gift, Dylan?
Thomas the Tank Engine,
The first toy for you to share.

We already share so much together,
So much love, so many of us,
This happy day!

20 January 2009

For Dorrie, From Her Son

We are together
Now.
Already we are sharing
Eternity.
The waiting and the troubles are over
For you.
My life has still to run its course
But your present experience
And my future
Are merging
In loving reminiscence.

For John Of The North

Sons of Cornwall,
Daughters of Cornwall,
Stand tall!

There is strength in your arms.
There is kindness in your eyes.
There is a heritage of Ancestral Wisdom in your veins.

And you will know your Creator

Through the songs of the Man
Whose voice is still heard among you.

On The Footpath To Sewardstone Marsh

…where year on year since his conception
A hundred autumns have scattered
Sun-dried oak leaves floating
Delicately on the flooded grassy way.

As a schoolboy
Did he vault this stile, run through this gate
Over the road homeward for tea
Where kerb-side topiary amazed
The waving Gypsy children in their caravans?

Did he, too, watch the hill from here
Where trees encroach across the skyline
Behind the house as Epping Forest nudges
Fields and farms down towards the reservoir?

Was this the make-shift ring where he out-boxed
The local bully? This the meadow where he swept
My mother off her feet to carry her across
The waist-high soaking corn
Oblivious in love?_ Legends that he would relate
To his wide-eyed young son on trips to sample
Bread and cheese and wood-smoke
And the hard-learned wisdom of his scouting lore.

Sandals And Boots

Down in Oxleas Wood the centurian stood
By the long, straight road where the Romans strode.
Up in Jolly Jack Wood the grandchildren stood
And the games they played as the tree trunk swayed
Recalled the climbs of the olden times.

Sam counted the rings on the trunks and things.
Ellen's broad smile made us dance for a while.
Ciara edged nearer where the leaves grew clearer.
Lulu and Roisin kept the branches in motion
Two of a kind with determined minds.
Chuckling Johnny, cheeks red and bonny,
Singing a song as we paddled along

In the mud and grass where the sandals passed
In an age long gone when the soldiers of Rome
Would rest on the hill as their children spilled
From the wagons to play on the tree trunk's sway
Finding acorns with roots where our Wellington boots
Would unearth the same in the years to come.

Spring-Green Spruce

New spring-green needles on the tips
Of upward-curving branches to the crown
For eighteen years this Christmas tree has spread
And grown with topmost branches taking turns
To arc alternately - a ballerina's hands.

A Norway spruce in alien surroundings year on year
Where once a tiny, potted evergreen
Was planted in suburbia on Twelfth Night
By teenage daughter number three
With great delight and pride and hope
As it survived and sprouted that first Spring.

Now round the tattered skirts dog violets hide
Brushed by the needles from the earlier days
And bluebell generations come and go.

Once holly berries from discarded wreaths
Took root and produced crimson in their turn
A prickly dark green backdrop to the stage
Where on her pointed toes the dancer longs

To stretch yet higher towards the lightening sky.
The Way We Were

Flies had buttons.
Trousers had braces.
Earrings had clips.
There were threepenny bits.
Ladies wore hairnets
And court shoes.
Toilet paper was shiny.
Plimsolls were for running.
Ice cream was a treat
With jelly for parties.

Christmas brought mistletoe
And paper chains, home-made.
Fireworks consisted of Vesuvius, jumping jacks
And boy scout rousers.
The tuck shop sold Spanish wood.
Coal was delivered
Down a hole in the step.
We counted the sacks
From behind the curtains.

Together

In many rooms
Where space and time are new
They are waking up together even now.
The history they knew, the order
Of departure and the memories
May be transformed.

'Again' may be a word there without meaning
In eternity's long curve beyond return.
'Waiting' may have reality in the life
Which has been left behind, but there…?

'Together' is the promised word.
You and I and we and they
And He. And His.
And the consequence of choice
In response to Love

24.8.1918

It was a Saturday
When Tom, my uncle died.
Eighty years later my mother still recalled
Her own mother's tears and the telegram.

August 1918
The Twenty-fourth, the print out says,
From the Website.

It was a Saturday.
Tom Merritt.
He was only twenty-two,
A Private in the Middlesex Regiment
With no known grave
But his name liveth for evermore

In the perpetual care
Of the Commonwealth War Graves Commission
The print out says

And of his God.

St Andrew's Day, 1969. An Edinburgh Festival

God comforted me at the High Kirk
My father was dying in London
Studies kept me in Edinburgh, that Sunday.
A sidesman welcomed me with kindness
The Knights of the Thistle were in procession for their annual service

Sir Robert Menzies, I remember, was among them,
The Premier of New Zealand.
It had been snowing and the brilliant winter sunlight
Made fractured diamonds of my falling tears,
As I returned to lunch,
Arthur's ancient seat on my left
Was gleaming white.
And my Iraqi student friends,
Learning about fisheries
Expressed sympathy.

You're 89, Mum

We've been for a drive.
Look at that sunset over the Autumn trees
And the children playing football
By the Jubilee Gardens of 1935.
Yes, it was sixty-four years ago,
You can certainly still do your mental arithmetic, but…
It's Tuesday, Mum.

You're 88, Mum.
You haven't been well.
A small stroke when they replaced the feeding-tube
That you had looked after so brilliantly living here alone.
We're just driving to the Nursing Home now.
It's Tuesday, Mum.

You're 87, Mum.
You've been to us for Christmas Day.
Yes, we're almost home. Remember moving in?
It was my seventh birthday, wasn't it?
Long enough ago for us both to remember.
It's Wednesday, Mum.

You're 90, Mum.
It was a good birthday, we all celebrated, didn't we?

Last night some of us went up to the Heath for the Millennium fireworks
Including your latest great-grandson.
This is the Hospital now, where you arrived in style on Boxing Day morning.
It's Saturday, Mum.

Paddy and I are with you, Mum.
I don't know if you can hear us now
As you slip away so quietly over the horizon.
It's Sunday, Mum.

Chapter 6

From London With Love

Bermondsey

At First Acquaintance

So now, it's nearly over
After all the years
People who told me everything
At first acquaintance.

Two minutes after handshake
('Take a chair. No, not that one')
The Tannoy invitation echoing in your ears
You started on your story.

What is a consultation? Two people
Talking about the illness of the one.
Sometimes reflecting back to me my own
So often beyond fiction in the facts of life.

Your symptoms, born of loneliness or stress
Tears not shed at bereavement, your dilemmas
May have had an answer in my creed
But your choices had of course to be your own.

Where were you born? It used to be upstairs
In S. E. 1 but now the answers come from all the Earth
Nigeria, Iraq, Somalia, The Caribbean
Hong Kong, Bolivia, Albania, Vietnam

Tehran, Kabul, Freetown, the list goes on
Dear birthplaces now lost in poverty or war or fear to you
The memories and living nightmares flood
Back with undeserved guilt for loved ones missing, presumed---?

But closer to home, the family occasion
Spoiled some twenty years ago, who now remembers why?
You've never spoken to them since
Nor ever will.

I saw your first smile, bonding with your Mum
You two shared all the world. Now she is here
With forms about your scholarship
The key to upward, onward hopes, mobility.

The paperwork, least said is best. These days
Computer windows open and the mouse
Alternates with clumsy typing
Before inwardly smiling gaze of youth.

Which leads to your tales of sex and drugs and Rock
And Roll and raves and morning after hangovers
And wasted days and years and tears and
Letters to the clinic and the wonderful counsellors.

And the Prince of Peace is waiting for the prayer
To open access to the love of God which never fails.
The question, 'Have you seen your priest about it?'
Maybe led to change.

' Plus ca change', boat people have voyaged on
East African Asians left the corner shops
Where families sold papers, bread and cigarettes
 Until Congestion Charges struck.

You toddlers, grown with children of your own
Have moved to leafy suburbs.
Inner City flats now house
Young traders burning out.
The Cypriot's fish shop died
(My on-call treat) but others of you queue
For pie' n' mash with liquor still.

Five helpings daily of salad, fruit and bran
Increasingly attract, however, and for once
I take my own advice in that respect.
No smoking, puffing, mobiles (' Please turn off')
Our rules in laminated notices
Sometimes would immortalise a typo,
'No animals allowed except blind dogs'
Nonetheless, welcome, stranger, to the team, primarily of care.

Whatever colour your convictions, orientation
Record or direction to your prayers
Just be sure to sober up before
Entering our ecumenical street door, by Methodists owned.

The quality of our services
('Why did you want this job?')
Has now been measured, targets met
At one small, recent point in time.

('What are your hobbies?')
We are rising to new challenges
As goal posts move, we are the 'keepers
('A ski instructor? Start today!')

May first acquaintance be remembered
Motivations, yours and mine, vocations
Post-code chance, or choice, so long ago
Brought us together.

Deptford

By Whose Authority?

The Bible is full of quotations
Inspiring many writers, one pen.
We interpret the meanings and wonders
In today's terms, but what were they then?

The context must be all-important
The first hearers, just what did they learn?
In their world without books or computers
They were open to feel their hearts burn.

Chorus
Read, think, now we must learn,
There is danger in ignorance, this is our turn.

Jesus certainly memorised Scriptures
The Pentateuch, Psalms and the rest.
And He told congregations with confidence
In the synagogues how they were blessed.

For He knew they had mastered the subjects
They already could quote all His texts
From childhood they'd lived with the precepts
Of authority, what would come next?

For He spoke with the power of wisdom
And the Spirit shone forth in His eyes
Which had seen, before time, fallen angels
And the lightning pre-dating the skies.

Chorus
Read, think, now we must learn
There is danger in ignorance, this is our turn.

Ukulele Rock

Ukulele Rock and Roll
Was good for his teenage mind and soul
With his walking, talking, living doll
He sang till broad daylight.

And it's ukulele Rock and Roll (x3)
He sang till broad daylight.

Banjolele Roll and Rock
Led the beat and the heartbeat round the clock
With his dustman's hat and the skiffle shock
On the bedpost overnight.

And it's ukulele Rock and Roll (x3)
On the bedpost overnight.

With the tap of the drumsticks uncle made
As the bachelor boy led the big parade
And the twisting dance will never fade
To the angel choir's delight.

And it's ukulele Rock and Roll (x3)
To the angel choir's de...
(A ukulele is an instrument
A hammer is a tool
At the Deptford Churches' Centre
We obey the Golden Rule)
To the angel choir's delight.

And that's Rock!

Ode To An Ode

I love your words and
Dedicated passion felt
In my sacred space.

Ode To A Toy Cat

Old lady, bereaved
In years gone by
Her cat lost,
Cuddles a soft toy.

'And Stay Out!...'

Slammed shut

Right in my face
To keep me out for good
My shadow trapped on the threshold
Knee high.

Ambiguity Rules Twice

A cave without a painting
A heart without a valve
A priest without a sainting
A wound without a salve
A tree with sap for tyres
A moon with face of cheese
A broadcast with no wires
What can we mean by these?

Blue Fingers...

...Icicles are mine,
Refrigerated wine
For me.
The white weather
Still holds together,
Jack Frost on the rooftops
Is waiting to see.

Thin sunshine
Rising past the hill,
Everything is still
And free
We're waiting for noon's
Rainbow blend
Of colours without end
And knuckles' cherry trend
And blue fingers
For me.

Cinquains From Art

Two trees
On the island
Hold a bottle of rum
Hanging in mid air. Yo Ho Ho.
Dead, man.

In space
Travelling light
Freelance cartographer
Has caught the to and fro in time
Frozen…

Van Gogh
Lend me your ear
You still have one to spare
Presenting your best side to the
Artist.

Crime Scene?

The door swung slowly open.
The hinges were creaking.
A sunbeam followed in my hesitant footsteps
And gradually my eyes became
Accustomed to the gloom.

They huddled together before I had spoken
As if they had never heard me speaking.
Their shadows were stilled against the fire-screens
And mistily their breath was seen
Suspended in the mystery of the room.

Desert Island Discos

(Those who can count five
Syllables and then seven
Will hear three Haikus…)

Where is Roy Plomley
When we need him most? Islands
Full of strange sounds. Men

Who chose music to
Eat by …Plus a stand-up act.
We were not rescued.

Hope

'Daddy'
Her first word
A symbol for a person
Call it out and he will arrive
'Abba, Father'.

Hurricane Cheryl Hits Deptford

Downpour, frown more, sounds roar
Car swishes, near misses, 'Sorry, missus!'
Wet feet, next sleet, eyes meet
Smiles rueful, two shoes full, socks awful
Trousers clinging, mud slinging, still singing.
Like to dance? Fat chance. Swift glance
Tears falling, stone walling, keep calling
Sounds fading, feet wading, sun's parading.

Journey Through the Centre
Softness of wall- to- wall carpeting.
Laminated notice. 'Please Ensure…'
Cigarette smoke climbs the stairs towards us.
Pork, cooking.

Red warning on the window, back-lit by the sun.
Voices raised in polite conversation.
Rough, white wall
Along the lobby.

Shuffling slippers by the servery
Among shadows overlapping on the floor.
Cold metal trolley.
Cabbage, cooking.

Warm sun, cool breeze.
Distant music over the grass
Wigwam pattern of poles
Between chives.

Saucepans rattle
The graffiti
Behind the kitchen
Potatoes, cooking.

Meridian At Nightfall

The laser shines from Greenwich
Downhill, green and brilliant through the dusk
Due North, where does it end?
Where is the pot of gold?
And does it glow?

The beacon light speeds well from Deptford
Uphill, striving through the dust
Due East, where will it reach?
Where does the anchor hold?
How can we know?

My Deptford

…is a man called Legion.
He is the wreckage of the past
And the hope for the future.
He has been offered minor surgery
When he needs a transplant.
He needs to help himself
And to grasp the offered hand

Outstretched to share with him
Inner transformation.

Rose in full bloom

Behind the dusty trees
Fulfilling prophecies from early Spring
But fading as I feel the
Autumn breeze.

A Doorstep On A Roman Villa

Worn by centuries of sandals
Remaining when the walls
Have largely disappeared.
'Ave', I say as I step across
Hailing the forgotten generations
Who lived and loved
And had their being here.
In this space, the atrium,
Hallway to home,
They greeted each other,
Shared the grapes of celebration,
Secure behind their much-loved
Doorstep.

Six Characters In Search Of An Emotion

'The ghost train disappeared into the gloom…
What was that shriek? What brushed my face?
What is that cold hand on my neck?'

'Another lovely dawn, the sun breaks through,
God is in His Heaven and lifts my heart,
With blessings warm and shared, no more alone'.

'Why did you interrupt my train of thought?
I almost had the answer in my grasp.
Now it is gone, I'll never know the truth'.

'Hello, hello, hello, what have we here?
Come in, old son, drink up, there's lots of time,
We'll have a laugh, stay on and on and on…'.

'Ho hum, a humdrum day,
I'm bored, no prospect of a new idea.
I think I'll just go back to…'

'Where, where can I look
Without regrets
And dreaming of what might have been?'

The Art Room And The Senses

I see cardboard boxes lying in wait on top of the cupboard.
The taste of strong tea lingers still
As we enter the closed room's musty odour.
My fingers discover the gloss of the formica table
With the matt of old paint smudges.
The only sound is the thoughtful tapping of biros.

The Door To Number 47

The stained glass birds
In two circular panels. Invisible
In the dark, to a ten-year-old
Latch-key boy
Stumbling at the second step
Across the coal-hole,
By the laurels I would later
Cut for my house-bound mother,
And the towering privet.

The door-knocker, looming,
Causing panic.
Our teacher had just read us
 'A Christmas Carol'.
I saw the face of dead Jacob Marley.

The Gifts

If I could, I would give to you
A glade of bluebells in the Spring
The Autumn gloaming on a Scottish hill
Summer haze when the sun is king
Crisp, white snow in the Winter's chill
High, white clouds in a sky of blue.

Through His Pockets

Legion by name, his possessions were many
But of little value. Old coins, pennies
And three-penny bits.
String, just in case.
A Swiss Navy knife, quite uncommon
With its well worn cork-screw.
A scrap of paper with important messages
From the voices.
For the rest, only stones
From the river.
Ballast, should he feel like
A final dip.

Kidbrooke

Every Millennium Eve, It's Just The Same

You can never park in Kidbrooke
It's the donkeys that I blame
Every Millennium Eve, it's just the same.

Why aren't Kidbrooke folks considerate
Ever since the Romans came?
Every Millennium Eve, it's just the same.

You'll be sleepless in Kidbrooke
From the fireworks and the flame
Every Millennium Eve, it's just the same.

Champagne corks that litter Kidbrooke
Always give away the game
Every Millennium Eve, it's just the same.

Kidbrooke

The Morden College clock chimes on the hour
And Wricklemarsh in frost divided lies,
St James's Church sits snugly, spire on tower,
Observing Shooter's Hill to eastward rise.

For twenty years and more we've worshipped here,
Two daughters' wedding bells rang in delight,
A mother's funeral one winter clear
Beneath the sunshine's stained glass discs of light.

Four daughters knew this place, in choir and crèche,
Making their choices hither or beyond,
Their efforts and ambitious thoughts to stretch
And one grand-daughter baptized at the font.

We Don't Have Bonfires

We don't have bonfires ever any more.
The brambles moulder in unwanted silage.
Compost feeds on leaves of beech and cob
While nuts and branches re-join in the bin.

We don't burn holly on the thirteenth night
The crackle and the spit of bursting berries .
Christmas wrapping paper carefully stored
Will serve for birthday gifts throughout the year.

We don't toast pink marshmallows any more
The sticky knitting needles children's hands
Clutched till they became too hot to hold
With whispering giggles, eyes round in the glow.

We don't make charcoal from the apple twigs
The pie-smell roasting rotten peel and cores
Creating cauldrons in the red log caves
Will fade to memory's ashes dry and grey.

We don't have dying bonfires, though, in mind.
The flames that we remember, yellow and red
Carry colour coding year on year
When Kerria and roses, pruned, dead-headed, bloomed.

And smarting eyes are smiling through the smoke
Where intimacy sharing family warmth
Remains in cherished thoughts of seasons gone.

And Again I say, Recycle

We have a passion for recycling
Every Friday students call
To remove assorted cardboard
Leaning neatly by the wall.

Christmas cards, birthday and Easter
Greetings from the year that passed
Lovingly received, acknowledged,
All return to pulp at last.

Pulp to pulp, ashes to ashes,
Past their sell-by dates, employed
One more time to bear a message,
Uselessness again enjoyed.

Glass and paper, cans and plastic
Each fulfils a destiny
Resurrection, second living,
Newness from parsimony.

Stewardship of Earth's resources,

Waste not want not globally,
In our corner faith not vision,
World-wide change starts here, with me.

Crescendo

Garden Fireworks in order on a board in the out-house
Starting with a sparkler in an incandescent curve
Now a Roman Candle with a plop-plop, bursting
Of the dazzling coloured fireballs in the mist between the trees.
Then a rocket whooshing from the lighted blue touch-paper
The patter of the falling stars across the London sky.
The movement to finale brings a boy scout rouser
And the stunning of the eardrums with the power of a BOMB.

The anticlimax ending in the deafened total silence
Would display the empty bottle, burned-out cardboard tubes_
And home.

London's Water-colour Air

Water-colour autumn sky and park,
The gallery at Dulwich , water-colour outside and within
The genius of a Turner is still needed here
To immortalise the softness of the scene in broad wash light and dark,
The russet maple leaf, the curving climbing road
Where trees, mature in confidence,
March past the Chapel to the College of God's Gift
Where once I walked the day I was confirmed.

How could I know that forty-six years on
A mellowed and contented couple here
Would stroll and share the beauty of the day
Again in London's water-colour air
From vivid tropic sun in Singapore
And Persia's desert mountains clear and sharp?

Chapter 7

Journeys

A Family Of Adopted Oak And Pine...

...Planted together by a kindly hand
Whether of human or a higher design
Here thrived upon the rocky outcrop, planned
A future free of monarchy and fear
Withstanding storms from the prevailing wind
From far away to South or East of here.

An ill-assorted couple and their line
But cheek by jowl in love of sky and land
And mountain, lake-side, conversation, wine
Planting around themselves a garden, fanned
To life by dedicated shelter, where
Offspring and friends could flourish, heart and mind
But one by one lost foothold, still held dear.

Footnote: An allegory on Wordsworth and Coleridge.

At The Ramblers' Tea Room

Well, I have been rambling
After a fashion
In my light raincoat
Flat cap
M & S trousers
And city boy's black leather shoes
Replicating past generations
Of my school uniform.

The plastic bag contains the Sunday
Newspaper, damp from urgent drafting
Of several poems in the rain.

I deserve my strawberry ice cream
As I write this on the serviette.

I... HAVE... been rambling.

Beware Of The Chickens...

...Beware of the hens
Beware of the ducks
And their feathered friends
Beware of the turkeys
They'll gobble you up
For I am only
A Doberman...pup.

His Environment

Squirrel who sits on a dry stone wall
Holds an immature acorn, a premature fall.
He darts through the traffic to avoid my gaze
A country-born squirrel
In a diesel haze.

A Paphos Trilogy

1. **Tell me, Paul.**

Did it strike you as ironic
Landing on the shore
That Aphrodite had emerged
From that same beach, some time before?

2. **Apostolic Succession**

If Aphrodite
Had been so mighty
Why did she pall
Before St Paul?

3. Inter Faith Dialogue

Lady,
If you're a goddess,
I'm no saint.

Points Of View

Tidy farms with tidy hedges
Past the window seem to glide
I am still, they are in motion
Tidy hedges in the wild.

Why should I mind juxtapositions
Man-made visions as I ride?
Tidy farms with tidy hedges
Seem to disturb my inner child.

Shadows On The Sands

Overhead sunshine casts moving stark shadows
Alum Bay chair lift ascending, descending.
 'Lift up your feet, love, I'll fasten the safety bar'
Dangling sandals in danger of falling,
Cliff faces crumbling, the sand in the bottles,
Sands of all colours hold shadows of angels
Rising and falling in Jacob's stone dreamland
Ladder to Heaven inspiring a patriarch.

Roundabout horses in circumscribed motion,
Fairground machine guns, stand clear of the ricochets,
Rockets and boatmen, gun placements and searchlights,
Marconi's message first heard here in Morse code.
Eyes of the Needles lie under the lighthouse
Sands of all colours hold shadows of angels.

Since The Year of The Flood…

…The moss grows on the South side.

Dead water-weeds are braided on branches
Chest high at the water's edge
Matted hair
On a medieval hangman's handiwork.

Flotsam farther up the bank
Shows the high tide mark of that year
And on the beach
Oblivious
The late summer ripples are lapping on the stones
Between this season's grasses.

St. Denys' Sundial

The sundial standing full to view
Engraved with '1692'
Upon the shining face sublime
Is telling British Summer Time.

Three centuries have passed, fifteen
More years have registered between
The dial, set now at ten to three
And honey, early, still for tea.

The 11.15 From Didcot Parkway

All of a dash
Past close-cropped fields
On a plain with a frame
Of irregular, untidy hills
Back-lit
By the December sun.

The Jurby Deodand

Jurby, West Manx coast, stones upon the sand
Shell seeking, strolling, reaching out a hand
I found a pebble, large and round and bland.

This object seemed unusual, washed of sand
It settled like a weapon in my hand
The thought occurred, was this a deodand?

A kilogram that time forgot, the sand
Had ebbed and flowed, shaping it to the hand
That once used it to kill, a deodand.

What nonsense, it was beauty from the sand
Ideal for my distant garden, hand
Picked to display, no fearsome deodand.

We drove on around the northern coast, the sand
Changed colour, Maughold crosses came to hand
The holy stones carved out at His command.

The picnic done, from Maughold Head the sand
Once more invited my exploring hand
But what if I possessed a deodand?

Descending. Cursed? The skies grey on the sand
I once more took this stone in my right hand
And weighed the merits of a deodand.

It had to be returned. The eastern sand
Of Port Mooar was welcoming my hand
I gently hid the guilty deodand.

Geologists in future, dating sand
With yet- to- be- invented scans in hand
 May puzzle at my displaced deodand.

But out of place and time this stone will stand
Meet cleansing restitution at His hand
And truly serve, a holy deodand.

What Did You Go Out To See?

Down past 'The Green Man' and 'The Olde Smithy'
Avoiding the fractured stile and a few remaining puddles in the lane
Where July sun has dried the surface gravel
I pause to pay attention to the breeze
Coaxing the individual melody from thorn and oak
Pollarded ash and hazel hedge.

To the right, pea-pods in shy and serried ranks
Are ripening.
Opposite, the blackberry and ivy curtains part
To reveal an expanse of grain, whose rustling wave-forms
Accompany the bull-rushes.

What did you go out to see or hear?
A reed blown by the wind?

Or a small pond where unknown fish
Gulp at the limit of their world for flies;
A rubbish pile of cartridges spent in last Sunday's quest
For sport, not food; the stricken remains
Of clay pigeons, orange, brittle, splintering
Which crunch beneath my shoes along the wayside grass.

Further on, as I skirt the stony fields of wheat
Between the neo-Gothic, head-high arches
Formed by graceful, errant last year's oats
A bird of prey rides on the rising warmth
Alert for signal, sight or sound, before a sudden dragon-fly
Rasps through dead stalks to join the air display.

The distant traffic hums its background chorus
And a tethered horse two meadows away provides a solo.
Then all subsides as butterflies red, brown and white
Whisper together upon the purple thistle flowers.

World Cup, Japan, 2002

World Cup, Japan, a football thrill.
Will England score the golden goal?
But our goalkeeper has had a spill.

Classical maestros from Brazil,
They take their corner kicks with soul.
World Cup, Japan, a football thrill.

Twenty-third minute psalm: one-nil.
The semi-final drums may roll
But our goalkeeper has had a spill.

Rivaldo's forty-seventh skill
Will equalise the half-time toll.
World Cup, Japan, a football thrill.

Ronaldhinio makes the kill
His sending-off then leaves a hole
But our goalkeeper has had a spill.

With breakfast untouched on the grill
England the'keeper can't console.
World Cup, Japan, a football thrill,
But our goalkeeper has had a spill.

The Visitor And The Madonna

The heavy door swung open for him
The visitor's eyes began their pilgrimage,
Inside the Cathedral of Santa Maria
The September sun faded in reverence.
The afternoon palms of Fuerteventura became a memory
For this was Betancuria
Site of tragedy.

A Franciscan monk's statue stood by the Bishop's chair

With statues of Santa Maria.
Do not touch the statues.
The statues did not touch the visitor.
Save one.

The sad Madonna, in black, elevated to be carried
By successors to the Six Hundred faithful
Enslaved by marauding Berbers.
He caught her eye, the downcast gaze a spotlight
Of spiritual sadness and desolation.
For centuries their eyes met in empathy.
His openness to the bereaved, her inexpressible grief,
The key and the lock.

Her eyes, created to contain a world of loss,
His total offering of himself;
Did she weep, so full of life and longing?
The wood was dry.
His were the tears that flowed
For both of them.

Twelve Stone Blocks

The quarryman stood by his broken saw.
The circle was twisted, the teeth were raw.
Eleven blocks perfect as a mason's dream
But the twelfth was warped by a hidden seam.

For the limestone wall under Malta sun
In the deepening quarry as each day was done
Stood smooth and gleaming with the straight cut scars
Horizontal and vertical to greet the stars.

But the twelfth white block with the warping seam
Malformed by the long-dry underground stream
Was crooked and hard, resisting the hand
That had sought to shape as the mason planned.

And the priest in the village after Mass was said
Reflected on the vision of the twelfth block, dead
To the hand of the Master as eleven blocks dried
Living stones, responding as the mason tried
To create an altar for the church on the hill
With one block lost to a stubborn will.

Orzola Harbour

Fishing boats facing towards the tide
Fluttering pennants in the evening sun
Incoming breakers at the harbour wall
Flat, gutted fish with mirror image eyes
Pegged out on lines like bunting to dry.
The 'Graciosero Uno'
Submarine vision out of Las Palmos
Snarls with painted fangs silently ashore.
Tourists surfeited with glass-bottomed wonders
Seek the steadying influence
Of the bottom of a glass.

Chapter 8

Earlier...

The Golden Arrow

The golden train speeds down the line
A flash of light and then it's gone.
Its golden paint looked very fine
Oh how it glistened .Oh how it shone.
At last it's reached it's destination
And pulls in to Dover station.

Just like that is the life of a man
A flash of light and then it's gone
As onward to his home he ran
Oh how it glistened , Oh how it shone.

At last he's reached his destination
And his heart filled with elation.

(written at age 11)

A Small Bereavement
(June 1999)

A sudden, stupid absence. An empty chair.
There it was, gone. Lost, stolen or strayed.
The Bag.
'Bluish, greenish brown it was, sergeant.
We only left it on the chair while we cleared up the Marquee.
Nothing valuable, no, only clothes.
The clothes my wife needed for the evening

Without which our plans had to be
 Abandoned.'

I felt ambiguous about that bag.
A hearty dislike might come closer.
I could never do it up.

Am I in denial?
'I never liked it, I'm glad it's gone'?
There was certainly anger, guilt and resentment.
All the elements of bereavement are here,
Including the sympathy of friends.

It had been a religious do.
We had sung, 'This Is My God, The Servant King'
With a lump in the throat. Mine, at least.
We had been clearing the detritus of the saints
When the bag-shaped void appeared.

I hope you like your new-found property, dear sir or madam;
My favourite Oxfam cap and Cancer Shop sweater, too large.
The pot of yoghourt left from lunch.
The prescription sun-glasses of hers
Useless to others. Her jacket matching the remaining skirt.
The photos of the grandchildren, unshared.

Each item significant
Only to us. Now yours. Plus a few paracetamol
And a letter from a missionary. Enjoy.
But please, God, can we turn back time?

(This poem led to a new start in creative writing)

Wine and Incense - A Love-Offering.

I long to live my life in rhyming couplets
Exposing my true feelings now to view
From the overflowing cup of blessings, droplets
Pouring out received libations here to you.

I wish I had facility for rhythm

And rhyming climbing breathlessly for air
From the depths of my unconscious thoughts and with them
Offering incense as a symbol we can share.

With humility I dare to risk the blighted
Results of my aspiring to inspire
With similes both separate and united
Wine or water, love, smoke, poetry or fire.

Acrostics

Can I do this?
How should I start?
Retirement, a beginning not an end.
Is there life before death?
Shall we find out
Together?
Or
Perhaps
Hear the truth today, about
Eternal
Rest.

Dust
Everywhere
Paralysed
Traffic
Fuming.
Overhead, the light
Railway to
Docklands

Beside The Traffic's Roar

…A silent promise that the Summer will not pass
Unheeded as I dream behind my door

Daughter Of The Totem

In the Yorkshire Sculpture Park where
Moccasin has never trodden
Stands a totem in the Parkland
In the rolling Yorkshire Parkland
Where the rain falls on the tea room
And the sun shines on the tourists
Glares an eagle from the totem
Painted brightly near the oak trees.

As I stood there with my daughter
By the totem in the Parkland
She was given words of wisdom
Words explaining inner meaning
How the tribes adopted eagles
And the creatures of the forest
Representing ancient virtues
Qualities shared with the creatures.

Meanwhile elsewhere in the meadows
Henry Moore's reclining sculptures
Well concealed their own intentions
And their reasons for creation
Unlike creatures of the forest
Giving birth to deep traditions
Bequeathing qualities to humans
With perception, like my daughter.

Dearest Clone- A Mother's Promise

My daughter, your transparency is showing
My sister, I can read your tiny mind
In dreams I see your teenage cheeks are glowing
At your bedside my own memories I find.

To bridge your troubled soul while you are growing
To smooth your way of obstacles I knew

In waters deep and still, not overflowing
Your life I'll guard, our instincts will be true.

No tide will drown you while I span the ocean
No abyss of fear to swallow or to hold
No man will threaten, flooding with emotion,
My love is yours to strengthen and enfold.

Your stepfather has left us close together
To be your brother-in-law he could not bear
Enough to know being all to one another
One flesh shall be our certainty to share.

Skin of my skin, blood of my own creation
Heart of my heart and bone cell of my bone
Our future holds the founding of a nation
One mind, bridge, anthem, children of the clone.

Extra-ordinary

Have you seen the wallpaper along the halls of time?
Or have you heard the Muzak of the spheres?
Double glazing has been guaranteed across the glassy sea
And the everyday will last a thousand years

Have you felt the particle approach the speed of light?
Or the quark that passes painlessly through Earth?
From Antarctica to Kandy nineteen seconds have elapsed
Strangely warming Gaia' s cockles to new birth.

There is meaning in the Universe for those with eyes to see
And with ears to hear the harmony complete
Mathematics, music and the paint that never dries
On the flowers that bloom forever at your feet.

From Life

My body in its seventh decade

Reflects the likeness of a Rembrandt nude
An etching, who would come upstairs to see?
His red chalk lines would emphasise rotundity
Of abdomen, brown ink the shrinking muscle
of my limbs.
The copperplate would state

The mirror image truth,
The feet that used to dance, the fists to box, the broken tooth.

No oil painting, but art would come to aid
And create images of beauty viewed
Through eyes that dare to chance in me
Interpretations of profundity
An inner meaning, youth with age would jostle
For expression, strive for man's estate.

Give Us Today

May we be close today, you and I
My heavenly Father, here on Earth with me.
Through Son and Spirit may we see
My friends and neighbours as your family.

May we be hungry today, you and I
Hungry for justice, righteousness and love
Longing for feeding from above
With the Living Bread, under your loving eye.

May we be thirsty today, you and I
My crucified Lord, risen, walking with me
Thirsty and knowing reality
Sharing suffering with those who pass by.

Haiku 1 - Sam, About Tom

The good doctor said
Of the poet Gray,

'He is dull, in a new way'.

Haiku 2 - Alpha To agemO

At the end of days
Universes will implode
Not bangs but srepmihw

Haiku 3 –Encounter

On our Paphos Beach
Aphrodite, my poor love,
You will meet St. Paul.

In All Its Fullness

A day full of prayer
A night full of grace
With hearts full of blessings
In each sacred space.

A life full of peace
A song full of praise
When, filled by the Spirit,
We rejoice full of days.

Ingrate

I remembered to pray, 'Please'
Before seeing
The Consultant.

But I forgot to pray, 'Thank you'
Until after seeing
The Pharmacist.

Pearls Or Beads

'Life is a string of pearls, my child,
With tiny ones at either end.
You are not as important yet
As older children. You prepare
For great things in the future
And must long for more fulfilment as you grow
And learn and save and hope and pray
For stature, status, understanding, wit and recognition.

There will come a time when all
Is optimum, achieved, today the crown, the largest pearl
But what you can expect to follow on
Will be diminishing returns
Capacity of thought and stamina reducing
Going, going, almost gone.'

'No, father, life is just a string of beads,
My nursery days as precious as my school,
Time to enjoy my gifts as day by day
They change, not grow, no judgement must be made.

Each day is equal, twenty-four long hours
Though pleasure or excitement makes them speed.
Please don't ignore me now that I am young
Just put your newspaper aside and share
My wonder at the new things I can learn.
Perhaps you too will through my eyes acquire

The simple knowledge of a day well spent
In being just myself, playing not doing,
Reading together, walking in the park,
The bedtime story – Each may be our last.'

Plane Trees...

Bearing little asteroids

Black silhouettes
Against the leaden promise
Of the morning firmament.

Poetry In The Rain

When Soph was there and Matt and you
Mid Summer was on its way
We had a Yorkshire holiday one wet and windy day.
The picnic by the riverside we ate beneath a tree
And I read you my poems, a captive audience of three.
'Write them in your sketch book', was my family's advice
'Then they can be a record of your trips, recorded twice'.
So I'm writing this beside the drawings of the hills again
In memory of a happy day and poetry in the rain.

Post Meridiem

My poetry
Helps to steady me
In the centre of spirituality.
My penitence
In the present tense
Brings awareness of God's omnipotence.
My garden times
As the sun declines
Makes me warmer than any Persian wines.
As I near the end
And I need a friend
Rhyme and reason give way to the love you send.

Rydal

Please drive carefully
Through our village.
There are poets about.
They are wandering lonely
But have no doubt
They have heard you coming

They are eagle-eared
But they're looking at the clouds
And they know no fear.

Sequel

1914,1939,2003.
Flickering subtitles
Warning future audiences what is to come.
Will these be the World War years
Familiar to surviving script writers and poets, if any?

Set Aside...

...or just neglected?
A nice little earner
For an exhausted farmer?
Or the guilty evidence
Of the neighbouring pensioner's
Disability?

Shimmer

On the June tarmac, early mourners watch
A shimmering above the chimney shadow
Cast by municipal decorative brick.
The crematorium looks different in the Summer.
Most visits have been Winter chest infections' work
On relatives in old age.
This friend had battled death
For months until the roses bloomed
And how they bloomed in riotous hush
Flourishing gratefully in memory
Of their distant scattering past.
Generations of roses and benches have been tended here
By sons' and daughters' hands across the years
And widows of the good and loved
Have alighted through the shimmer on the tarmac.

These Are The Days

Once upon a time there was a stable
When the Lord was born the angels knew
How they filled the sky with songs of glory
To think of all the great things he would do

Chorus:
These are the days, my friend
We know they'll never end
We'll praise the Lord for ever and a day
To live his life we'll choose
His love we'll never lose
These are the days, my friend, these are the days.
Alle Alleluya, Alle Alleluya, Alleluya Alle Alleluya

Soon the thirty years flew swiftly by him
Came the time to teach and heal the crowd
But the friends he loved would soon deny him
Crucified, in death his head was bowed

Chorus

On Easter Day they came into the garden
Sadly they would say their last goodbyes
But the angels once again were joyful
And Jesus soon appeared before their eyes

Chorus

Soon we all will come to him for judgement
See his face and hear him call our name
Glory, Father, Son and Holy Spirit,
For in our hearts the song is still the same

Chorus

Train Journey

As I walk forward through the moving train
Along the corridor of uncertain length
Every compartment is different and some less important.
I may speed up to reach the buffet car
Or long to see the driver
Forgetting or discounting
The shaky route through empty carriages
Just seen as ground prepared for those ahead.

Suddenly I become aware
Of an out of the body experience.
I can see the train entire from above.
From guard's van to engine it snakes below me
As from the moment after death life can be seen complete
With every day deserving equal honour.

Vocation

'The words just flow', the chairman said when choosing me as speaker
But extemporary speaking made the evening meeting weaker
For the audience was scientific, medical and old
And experience of charismatic Persia left them cold.

But that's not true, for one or two expressed appreciation
There were murmurings exuding sympathetic approbation
For my tale of Middle Eastern nightingales and revolutions
Narrow misses, mountain passes, problems finding no solutions.

I didn't use transparencies or have extensive notes
My wife and I had found the goulash stick within our throats
At the introduction dinner with the black- tie- clad committee
In my borrowed dinner jacket rushing from the inner city.

For it wasn't my vocation to be feted, wined and dined

I preferred to be in solitude and seeking peace of mind
As the trauma was too recent of that terrible return
From the murder of our priest and friend and seeing Shiraz burn.

When Will They Ever Learn?

They march away into the mists
Of time
The soldiers out of another age
From mine.
The bugle calls, they break into
A run
The bayonet, claymore, pointed stick
And gun
Are levelled at a dimly perceived
Foe
One of the Others whom they cannot
Know

Your Early Morning Call

I'll never be ready for work
If the muse continues to call
When the poetry flows at breakfast time
And my spirit's oblivious to all.

So, quickly, write it down
Before it flies away,
In the morning chorus of things to do
In the clamour of everyday.

Acknowledgements And Notes

Chapter 2

Incarnate! : Previously entitled 'Identification' this poem arrived in 2000 and was introduced by Margaret Silf at the Dominican Convent, Greenwich.

Beyond The Decorations: Part of a presentation given in 2005 by the author at the Dominican Convent, 'Poetry And Prayer For Advent'.

Good Morning... The next five pieces were used at a Service of Holy Communion to help introduce a new liturgy.

Karaoke Christmas: Written in anticipation of the organist's absence.

Reunion: To commemorate the final act of worship at the closure of Crowther Hall, the CMS Training College in Birmingham.

The Ballad Of Joe And Mary Church: Based on an Advent sermon by Leslie Hocking, Reader at St. James's Church, Kidbrooke.

The Emptying: Inspired by the theological term 'kenosis', St. Paul's Epistle to the Philippians, chapter 2, verses 7 and 8.
The Knife Edge: Autumn 2001, following 9/11, in response to rumours of war.

The Night The Poetry Caught Fire: A true story, published in 'A Heart For Mission' (2006); featured in 'The Sign', the nationwide Church magazine supplement (December 2005) and in 'The Poetry Church Winter Collection' (2003).

The Perfect Day: For several years the proceedings of the Men's Group at St. James's Church have been minuted in verse, based on the members' contributions, as in this poem.

Without Christmas: Written early Christmas morning, 2000.

With gratitude to all who have encouraged me in these eight years of Creative Writing: ; Rev Kim Hitch, Rector of St. James' www.stjames-se3.org.uk ; Sister Martha at the Dominican Convent; Margaret Silf; all at the 'Creative Arts Retreat Movement' [www.carmretreats.org.uk] ; and 'Create'[www.createarts.org.uk].

Chapter 3

A Heart For Mission: a hymn and prayer used in the Parish of St. James', Kidbrooke from Lent to Trinity 2005.

A Hill Of Beans For Peace: describes a service at St. Peter's Roman Catholic Church, Woolwich on 9 February 2003 prior to the Second Gulf War.

And A Middleton New Year: Every one of these poems that describes an event or situation is true. Every one that describes a spiritual experience or aspiration is as accurate as possible.

Before The Diagnosis: published in 'Sounding Heaven And Earth' (Canterbury Press).2004

Blueprint In The Sand: 'Poetry Church' Collection Summer 2004.

Day One: written on 20 March 2003 at the outbreak of the Second Gulf War.

Dear Colleague: reflections on a Christian workplace. 'The Poetry Church Collection' Summer 2005.

From Galilee To Here: 'The Poetry Place' 2005.

Hold That Word: appeared in 'Pilgrimages 2006', an anthology chosen from Christian poems published by 'Feather Books' in the quarterly 'The Poetry Church' between1995 and 2005.

God, Forsaken, A Meditation On Psalm 22: 'The Poetry Church' Spring 2006.

Hopton Wafers Churchyard: reflections written at my wife's family church.

How Was Your Day? A morning and evening prayer, the starting point being the Ignatian Examen.

Iran Morning: Church Mission Society magazine 'Yes',1975.

Lord, Teach Us To Pray: a hymn and prayer used at St. James' during Lent 2006.

Michaelmas: written on 29 September 2005 during a 'Poetry And Prayer' Retreat at Rydal House held by The Creative Arts Retreat Movement www.carmretreats.org The author has recently become a poetry tutor at CARM.

Prayer Tank: December 2001. Prayers for peace have continued regularly at St. James' since '9/11'. Featured in 'The Poetry Church' Summer 2003.

Taking The Oath: a prayer of re-dedication. 'The Poetry Place' 2005.

To See More Clearly: inspired by a Home Group involving stillness and meditation.

Yellow: written during a workshop held by the charity 'Create' www.createarts.org. for members and volunteers at The Deptford Churches Centre www.deptfordcc.co.uk

With gratitude to Rev. Kim Hitch and the congregation for

unfailing support as the poems arrived and were shared www.stjames-se3.org.uk; heartfelt thanks to Margaret Silf for writing the Foreword; also to colleagues and friends at Bermondsey and Lansdowne Medical Mission for their interest and enthusiasm. Above all, my warmest appreciation to my wife and family for their love, patience, practical help and encouragement.

Dedication: To my wife, Paddy, whose prayer, 'Give us, Lord, A Heart For Mission' on 24 January 2005 inspired the title poem and named the subsequent Church Renewal Programme in Kidbrooke.

Lightning Source UK Ltd.
Milton Keynes UK
UKOW05f1230230614

233897UK00002B/53/P